IMAGES of America

THE RICHMOND 34 AND THE CIVIL RIGHTS MOVEMENT

SCENE FROM INSIDE THALHIMERS DEPARTMENT STORE. Leroy Bray Jr. and Elizabeth Johnson are under the watchful eye of the police and Thalhimers authorities. (Courtesy of the University of Virginia Library.)

ON THE COVER: SCENE FROM THE RICHMOND SIT-IN. As police officers and bystanders look on, impeccably attired Virginia Union University student Leroy M. Bray Jr. waves to the crowd as he is about to be driven to jail on trespassing charges. (Courtesy of the Valentine History Center.)

IMAGES
of America

THE RICHMOND 34 AND THE CIVIL RIGHTS MOVEMENT

Dr. Kimberly A. Matthews
and Dr. Raymond Pierre Hylton

ARCADIA
PUBLISHING

Copyright © 2020 by Dr. Kimberly A. Matthews and Dr. Raymond Pierre Hylton
ISBN 978-1-4671-0451-7

Published by Arcadia Publishing
Charleston, South Carolina

Printed in the United States of America

Library of Congress Control Number: 2019949298

For all general information, please contact Arcadia Publishing:
Telephone 843-853-2070
Fax 843-853-0044
E-mail sales@arcadiapublishing.com
For customer service and orders:
Toll-Free 1-888-313-2665

Visit us on the Internet at www.arcadiapublishing.com

I dedicate this book to my parents, Albert and Lindell Matthews.

—KAM

To Mary Claire Hylton, Nicole DeVizcaya Hylton, Madeleine Henriet Marchal, Thomas Preston Hylton, Alice Henrietta Whitrow, and Eric Hugh Whitrow.

—RPH

Contents

Acknowledgments		6
Introduction		7
1.	Richmond and the Byrd Machine, to 1960	9
2.	Virginia Union University, to 1960	31
3.	The "Oil" on the "Flame," February 1–22, 1960	49
4.	The Campaign for Human Dignity, 1960–1963	71
5.	The Forgetting and the Rediscovery, to 2010	93
6.	The "34/50" Commemoration and Beyond, 2010–2019	103
Bibliography		127

Acknowledgments

The authors would like to give a heartfelt thank-you to those who shared their stories and photographs with us to preserve this small portion of African American history.

For encouragement and assistance with the creation of this book, the authors thank the following: Selicia Gregory Allen, Ray Bonis, Malcolm O. Carpenter, Luminita Dragulescu, Elliott Eddie, Reginald Ford, Katrice Hawthorne, Brianna Nikole Scott, Samuel D. Taylor, and Peter Wallenstein. Deep thanks to Caroline Anderson and the team at Arcadia Publishing.

Most of the images in this volume appear courtesy of the Library of Congress (LOC), the Virginia Union University Archives (VUU), the University of Virginia (UVA), Virginia Commonwealth University (VCU), the Valentine History Center (VHC), the Department of Historical Resources (DHR), the Office of the Governor of Virginia (GOV), and the *Richmond Times-Dispatch* (RTD).

INTRODUCTION

On February 22, 1960, Richmond City Police arrested 34 Virginia Union University students at the insistence of the Thalhimers Department Store management on the charge of trespassing. This was for sitting on chairs reserved for white customers and asking for service at the department store lunch counter and its Richmond Room restaurant. They, and other Virginia Union University students, were participating in the momentous sit-in movement, which had begun at a Woolworth's store in Greensboro, North Carolina, on February 1, 1960, and spread through the Upper South. Sit-in protests sprang up, one after the other, over the course of 19 days in Durham, Fayetteville, Winston-Salem, Charlotte, Concord, Elizabeth City, Henderson, High Point, Raleigh, Salisbury, Chapel Hill, and Shelby, North Carolina. The movement spilled over into other states: South Carolina (Rock Hill, Sumter, and Charleston); Florida (Tallahassee); Tennessee (Nashville and Chattanooga); and Virginia (Hampton, Portsmouth, and Norfolk). The Richmond sit-in began on February 20, 1960, and was the 23rd in succession. The groundwork had been laid in Richmond on January 1, 1959, by Dr. Wyatt Tee Walker, who was later chief of staff for Dr. Martin Luther King Jr. when he held a massive nonviolent prayer pilgrimage through the city.

The arrest of the 34 Virginia Union students was not only the largest mass arrest up to that time arising from a nonviolent civil rights protest, but sparked a peaceful boycott and protest movement—the Campaign for Human Dignity—and within slightly more than a year had virtually destroyed legalized racial segregation in the former capital of the Confederacy. The Richmond 34, as they would later be known, were found guilty of trespassing and fined $20, but the ruling was appealed, and on June 10, 1963, the Supreme Court overturned their convictions in the case of *Raymond B. Randolph, Jr., et al. v. the Commonwealth of Virginia*.

But the story encompasses more than 34 arrests and a court case. It is also the story of the city of Richmond and the state of Virginia, where these students dwelled and studied, and the university that educated them. In common with other Southern states brought back into the Union as a result of the Civil War, Virginia saw its government taken back after Reconstruction by Southern whites who harbored a deep resentment against both the federal government and African Americans. From the 1880s and well into the 1920s, the states of the former Confederacy had established systems based on white supremacy, racial separation, and political dominance by the conservative element of the Democratic Party. In Virginia, this governing clique was known as the "Byrd Machine" after governor and longtime US senator Harry Flood Byrd Sr. The state capital openly displayed its Confederate past and, in keeping with other Jim Crow systems throughout the South, mandated separate bus seating, restaurant and lunch counter seating, restrooms, bus waiting rooms, and schools, and criminalized interracial marriages.

Ironically, segregation itself sowed many of the seeds of its own destruction. The African American community, forced to draw upon its own resources, developed businesses, churches, and educational institutions that nurtured an increasingly strong black middle class. In Richmond, the core area was Jackson Ward. Eminent among the black educational institutions was Virginia

Union University. Among the oldest of the Historically Black Colleges and Universities (HBCUs), Virginia Union was founded in 1865 and by the 1950s had encouraged generations to take pride in their accomplishments, foster self-respect, and demand fair treatment from the society of which they formed an integral part. Unsurprisingly, the university produced many civil rights leaders and social activists, including Dr. Wyatt Tee Walker, Alice Jackson Stuart, Walter Fauntroy, Randall Robinson, Henry L. Marsh III, Spottswood Robinson III, Curtis Harris, Janet Jones Ballard, and, of course, the Richmond 34. Life in Richmond went on, the civil rights movement forged ahead, and the students graduated, moving forward with their lives, while their university went on to educate succeeding generations of students. Despite its considerable significance, the Richmond sit-in was largely forgotten, the details tucked away in fading newspaper archives and library microfilms. It was quickly overshadowed by subsequent, more dramatic events, and the focus of the civil rights struggle gravitated toward the Deep South states. The freedom rides; the Albany, Birmingham, Danville, Selma, and Cambridge, Maryland, movements; the March on Washington; the passage of the Civil Rights and Voting Rights Acts; and the Freedom Summer in Mississippi all demanded national attention and pushed many earlier, comparatively less turbulent events into the background.

A great deal of progress was made from the 1960s through the 1990s and beyond by Virginia's African American community, and breakthroughs unheard of in 1960 materialized: the chair of the Richmond City School Board; the Virginia House of Delegates and Senate; the mayoralty of Richmond; the lieutenant governorship; and the office of governor itself. On the national level, an African American presidential candidate twice carried once firmly segregationist Virginia. As for the 34 students themselves, apart from two exceptions, they were rarely mentioned, and it was not until a half century had passed that their names were engraved on a monument stone: Frank George Pinkston, Charles Melvin Sherrod, Elizabeth Patricia Johnson, Ford Tucker Johnson Jr., Celia E. Jones, Joanna Hinton, Randolph Tobias. Woodrow B. Grant Jr., Leroy M. Bray Jr., Wendell T. Foster Jr., Milton Johnson, Barbara A. Thornton, Albert Vann Graves Jr., Carolyn Ann Horne, Larry Pridgen, Gloria C. Collins, Patricia A. Washington, Ronald B. Smith, Joseph E. Ellison, Raymond B. Randolph Jr., Thalma Y. Hickman, Lois B. White, Marise L. Ellison, John J. McCall, Virginia G. Simms, Clarence A. Jones, Donald Vincent Goode, Gordon Coleman, Samuel F. Shaw, Robert B. Dalton, George Wendall Harris Jr., Ceotis L. Pryor, Anderson J. Franklin, and Richard C. Jackson.

Then, some 44 years on, a series of remarkable coincidences began to bring the incident back into the limelight. Since then, it has slowly been regaining recognition as the pivotal moment in history that it truly was. Much of what occurred afterward stemmed from the events of that February morning that are coming to the fore at long last.

One
RICHMOND AND THE BYRD MACHINE, TO 1960

On April 3, 1865, one chapter in history ended for Richmond when Federal troops marched in and planted the flag of the United States on the state capitol building. Richmond's time as the capital of the Confederacy was over, and so too was slavery in the city.

After a brief Reconstruction period, conservative Democrats and Lost Cause advocates reasserted their political control over state and municipal government, and by the 1890s, a white supremacist system combining racial segregation with minority disfranchisement was firmly rooted. From 1893 to 1960, a powerful conservative political machine, led first by Sen. Thomas S. Martin and after 1919 by Harry F. Byrd Sr. (governor from 1926 to 1930 and US senator from 1933 to 1965), exerted dictatorial control and maintained segregated schools, public facilities, restaurants, lunch counters, waiting rooms, and movie theaters.

In Richmond, the African American community established an enclave on the north side of the city called Jackson Ward, which thrived and prospered well into the 1950s. Though there was some progress in race relations in the aftermath of World War II, the grip of the Byrd Machine seemed strong as ever. From 1954 to 1958, the construction of Interstate 95 cut a swath that bisected Jackson Ward and diminished it as a community. In response to the 1954 Supreme Court ruling in *Brown v. the Board of Education*, the Byrd Machine defiantly launched its "Massive Resistance" campaign to maintain the status quo. Before suburban malls became popular, the strip of Broad Street stretching between First and Tenth Streets was known as "Exciting Downtown Richmond," and shoppers converged from far afield. It was clustered with department stores, restaurants, drugstores, specialty shops, movie houses, two bus stations, and barbershops, and was anchored by two swanky establishments: Thalhimers and Miller & Rhoads. In all these businesses, the color line was drawn, with black customers not allowed seating in white-only restaurants and lunch counters.

PART OF THE "BURNT SECTOR" OF RICHMOND, 1865. The Evacuation Fire of April 2–3, 1865, was set by retreating Confederate soldiers acting under orders of Gen. Richard S. Ewell to destroy the tobacco stores. A stiff wind sent it out of control, and 30 blocks of the city were engulfed, amidst chaotic scenes of fleeing residents and pillagers. Although Union troops marching into the city on the morning of April 3 had nothing to do with causing the fire, and even tried to keep it from spreading, embittered white Southerners could not be mollified in their resentment against what they viewed as the imposition of "Yankee" government. This festering hatred would help fuel a later backlash against the newly freed slaves and their descendants that would manifest in the infamous Jim Crow laws. (LOC.)

LINCOLN'S VISIT TO RICHMOND. Ignoring his advisors, who feared for his safety, Pres. Abraham Lincoln was determined to journey to the fallen Confederate capital and walk its streets one day after it had been liberated. Sailing upriver from City Point, the president, his 10-year-old son Tad, and a small Marine escort walked to the former White House of the Confederacy. Along the way, hundreds of freed slaves turned out to cheer him. Many white residents sullenly stayed in their homes but, contrary to fears, did not attempt to harm Lincoln. While the president's visit kindled hope for a better future for the four million emancipated African Americans, Lincoln himself had not much longer to live. Ten days later, on April 14, 1865, he was shot at Ford's Theatre in Washington by John Wilkes Booth and died the following morning. (LOC.)

FIRST AFRICAN BAPTIST CHURCH. As the oldest African American church in Richmond, its foundation dates to July 1, 1841. After Nat Turner's Rebellion in 1831, it was against state law for an African American to pastor a church or for black worshippers to assemble without a white person present. Not until after Richmond was liberated on April 3, 1865, was this restriction lifted, and shortly thereafter, the white minister, Dr. Robert Ryland, handed the pastorate to former slave James Henry Holmes. First African Baptist was joined by other black churches, such as Ebenezer and Sixth Mount Zion, to form one of the pillars of solidarity for the revitalized African American communities of Richmond. This photograph shows the church at its original site at College and Broad Streets. The congregation relocated to 2700 Hanes Avenue in 1955. (LOC.)

DEDICATION OF THE LEE STATUE ON MONUMENT AVENUE. On May 29, 1890, a statue of Gen. Robert E. Lee, the first in a series of Confederacy-inspired statuary on Monument Avenue, was unveiled with considerable fanfare. It was followed by likenesses of prominent Confederate figures: Gen. J.E.B. Stuart (1907), Confederate president Jefferson Davis (1907), Gen. "Stonewall" Jackson (1919), and Comdr. Matthew Fontaine Maury (1929). Coming during a period of history when the ultraconservative Virginia Democratic Party was solidifying its domination of Virginia politics and imposing racial segregation, the statues were a highly visible manifestation of the Lost Cause mentality, which sought to glorify the former Confederacy and foster white supremacy. The placing of a statue honoring African American tennis champion Arthur Ashe (1996) on Monument Avenue generated a heated controversy. The Confederate statues and their fate are the subject of an ongoing local and statewide debate. (VHC.)

DAVIS AND LINCOLN MONUMENTS. Statues, monuments, and differing opinions over the presentation and interpretation of history have been very much in the news recently. In Richmond, an intense community discussion arose over all monuments relating to the Confederacy, with a special mayor's commission recently proposing a "middle path" of taking down the Jefferson Davis statue on Monument Avenue and placing historical context notice on the others. Davis, a Mississippian, was deemed to have only a slight connection with Virginia. The decision of the National Civil War Museum to place a statue of Abraham Lincoln and his son Tad at the former Tredegar Iron Works site occasioned protests prior to its dedication on April 6, 2003. (Both, Dr. Kimberly A. Matthews.)

THOMAS S. MARTIN, 1847–1919. Born in Scottsville, Albemarle County, Virginia, Martin fought for the Confederacy and practiced law after the war. In 1885, he became active in politics as a conservative Democrat. In 1895, he was elected to the US Senate and served until his death. Martin brought into being the Democratic political organization that would control government in Virginia for nearly 70 years and would later be dubbed the "Byrd Machine." His organization ran on a very restricted franchise, including disfranchisement of African Americans through poll tax and literacy tests, and racial segregation. These components found their strongest expression in the Virginia Constitution of 1902, which Martin was instrumental in engineering. The 1902 constitution was not superseded until 1971, though the US Supreme Court declared some of its provisions to be unconstitutional prior to this. (LOV.)

VIRGINIA CHRISTIAN AND WILLIAM HODGES MANN. Virginia Christian (1895–1912) was a young African American woman in Hampton who worked for a wealthy white widow named Ida Belote. On March 18, 1912, Belote was found dead in her house, and Christian was arrested for murder. According to Christian's alleged confession, she struck Belote with a broom handle after her employer had first attacked her with a spittoon, never intending to kill her. Because of the trial's unusually rapid progress to conviction and capital sentencing, the defendant's youth, and evidence of past abuse of the defendant by Belote, a nationwide campaign for clemency was launched. Gov. William Hodges Mann (1843–1927), a Confederate veteran, declined to commute her sentence, and on August 5, 1912, Christian became the first female, and minor, executed in Virginia. (Both, LOV.)

JOHN MITCHELL JR. AND WALTER PLECKER. No two Richmonders better illustrate the racial divide during the early 20th century than John Mitchell Jr. (1863–1929) and Walter Ashby Plecker (1861–1947). Mitchell, the crusading editor of the *Richmond Planet* from 1884 to 1929, was indefatigable in combating racism, disfranchisement, and lynching. The inscription on his gravestone states that he would "walk into the jaws of death for his race." Contrastingly, Plecker was one of Virginia's most relentless white supremacists. As registrar for the Virginia Department of Vital Statistics from 1912 to 1946, he attempted to destroy the identity of Virginia's Native Americans by labeling them as "colored." An advocate of the Eugenics movement, Plecker helped write the Virginia Racial Integrity Act of 1924 and supported the Virginia Sterilization Act of 1924—roundly condemned by Mitchell and the *Planet*. (Right, LOV; below, RTD.)

HARRY FLOOD BYRD SR. AND BYRD STATUE AT THE STATE CAPITOL GROUNDS. Harry Flood Byrd Sr. (1887–1966) was elected to the Virginia Senate in 1915 and, after the death of Thomas S. Martin in 1919, rose through the ranks of the ruling conservative Democratic political organization and dominated it so, that it was renamed after him. Byrd served as governor from 1926 to 1930, and US senator from 1933 to 1965. Exerting almost total control over government at the local and state levels, Byrd maintained the Virginia Constitution of 1902, racial segregation and disfranchisement, and the 1924 laws on racial integrity and sterilization. After the *Brown v. the Board of Education* decision, he advocated "Massive Resistance" to integration of schools. His statue on the state capitol grounds was dedicated in 1976. (Left, VHC; below, Brianna Scott.)

JACKSON WARD AND 1935 RICHMOND MAP. The largest and most vibrant African American community in Richmond was Jackson Ward. Located roughly between Marshall and Hill Streets and extending to Belvidere Street in the west and roughly Third Street eastward in central Richmond, it teemed with shops, professional offices, theaters, hotels, restaurants, and nightclubs and was known as the "Black Wall Street" and the "Harlem of the South." At the Hippodrome Theatre on Second Street (right), artists like Duke Ellington, Count Basie, Cab Calloway, Bessie Smith, and Billie Holliday would visit and entertain the throngs assembling there. The 1935 map of Richmond denotes "Negro Settlements" in and around the city. (Right, Dr. Kimberly A. Matthews; below, University of Virginia Library.)

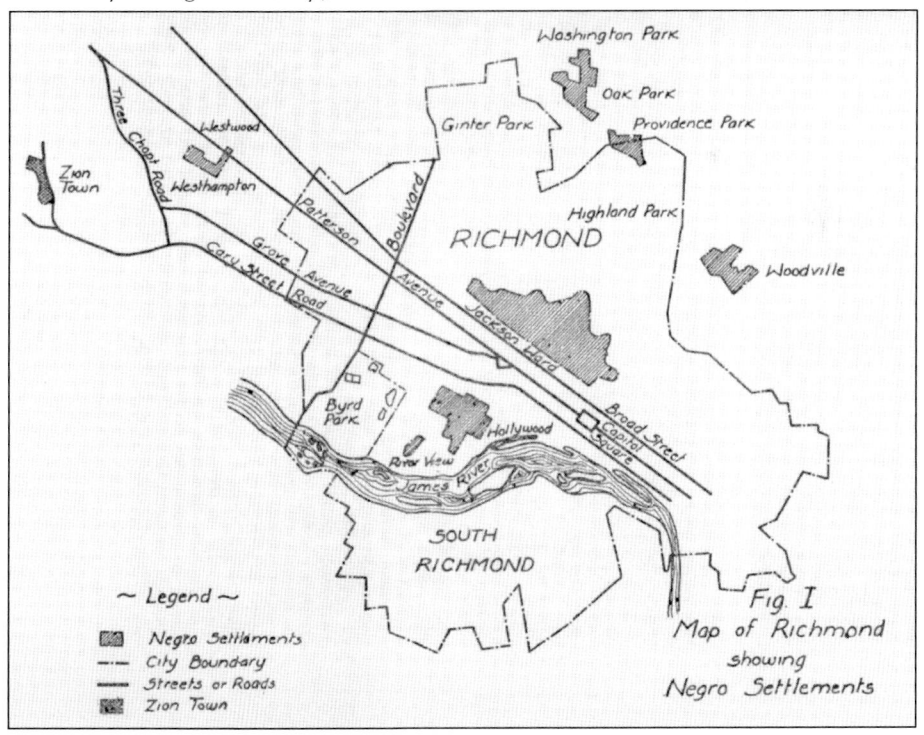

I-95 ROUTING THROUGH RICHMOND AND SIXTH MOUNT ZION CHURCH. The Federal Highway Act of 1957 created the interstate system but also had the consequence of destroying the Jackson Ward community. In a deliberate act of neighborhood destruction, the interstate split Jackson Ward just north of Duval Street, and the ward went into permanent decline, surviving only as a shadow of its former self. It was even planned to destroy the venerable Sixth Mount Zion Baptist Church, founded by free slave minister John Jasper. A vehement protest managed to save the church, and I-95 was routed to literally cut through its backyard. (Above, LOV; below, RTD.)

NAVY HILL: A COMMUNITY OBLITERATED. While remnants of Jackson Ward survived the debacle of highway construction, bulldozers, and backhoes, the black working-class district of Navy Hill did not. Navy Hill was named to commemorate the US naval victories over the British during the War of 1812, and its approximate boundaries extended east-west from Tenth to Third Streets and south-north from Leigh Street to Shockoe Cemetery. The district included Navy Hill School (above), established in 1871, which was the first school to employ African American teachers. But I-64, the Richmond Coliseum, and the Virginia Biotechnology Research Park all contributed to Navy Hill's complete destruction. There only remains a historical marker (right). (Above, LOV; right, Dr. Kimberly A. Matthews.)

KU KLUX KLAN MARCH IN RICHMOND AND SEGREGATION SIGNS. One fact that has long been forgotten is that from 1916 to 1925, the revived Ku Klux Klan (KKK) was a powerful political force and was not limited to the Deep South. Membership was openly flaunted, and at one stage, the Klan dominated the state governments of Indiana and Oregon. The above photograph shows a KKK parade through downtown Richmond in 1920. Though signs denoting segregated water fountains, restrooms, and park benches were in evidence, the Jim Crow system was more pervasive than that. It had become a way of life, mainly unspoken but widely understood. The signs were simply an outward manifestation of a mentality that would not change without a struggle. (Above, VHC; below, Virginia Commonwealth University Library.)

PRINCE EDWARD COUNTY: MOTON HIGH AND DR. KING. Virginia would prove to be crucial in the civil rights struggle, and it began to break in rural Prince Edward County. There, anger had been mounting over the blatant neglect of black schools, like R.R. Moton High School (above). Instead of relieving the overcrowding problem by expanding the school, the board of supervisors planted some cheap tar paper shacks. On April 23, 1951, the students responded by boycotting classes. From 1959 to 1964, the county supervisors closed all schools rather than integrate. Dr. Martin Luther King Jr. took a personal interest in the plight of Prince Edward's deprived students. Below, he is seen visiting and talking with them. (Above, Virginia Department of Historic Resources; below, Virginia Union University Library.)

GOVERNOR ALMOND. J. Lindsey Almond (1898–1986) served as the 58th governor of Virginia from 1958 to 1962. A product of the Byrd Machine, he defiantly echoed that organization's anti-integrationist sentiments and made fiery speeches proclaiming "Massive Resistance." However, in 1959, he did an abrupt turnabout, abandoning his segregationist stance and accepting desegregation in Norfolk and Arlington, Virginia. (LOV.)

POLL TAX RECEIPT. The Byrd Machine's favored method of voter exclusion was the poll tax. It had to be paid three years in advance as a prerequisite to voting and deterred many African American and poorer white citizens struggling to make ends meet. In 1966, the Supreme Court ruled the poll tax unconstitutional in *Harper v. the Virginia State Board of Elections*. (The Harrison family.)

BARBARA ROSE JOHNS. On July 21, 2008, the Virginia Civil Rights Monument, designed by Stanley Bleifeld, was dedicated on state capitol grounds. The front depicts Barbara Rose Johns, leader of the 1951 R.R. Moton High School student boycott. She and other students asked the National Association for the Advancement of Colored People (NAACP) for support, and attorneys Oliver White Hill Sr. and Spottswood Robinson III arrived on April 25, 1951. (Dr. Kimberly A. Matthews.)

DR. GRIFFIN. At the left side of the civil rights monument is a relief sculpture of Dr. Leslie Francis Griffin, pastor of the First Baptist Church of Farmville, Virginia, who galvanized community action in support of the student boycott. He continued to lead the civil rights movement in Prince Edward County through the school closure crisis from 1959 to 1964. (Dr. Kimberly A. Matthews.)

CIVIL RIGHTS LEGAL TEAM. Oliver White Hill Sr. (1907–2007) and Spottswood Robinson III (1916–1998) formed one of the most effective civil rights legal teams of the 20th century. Robinson earned his undergraduate degree at Virginia Union University before going to Howard Law School, while Hill attended Howard exclusively. Hill served on the Richmond City Council from 1949 to 1951 as its first black member since Reconstruction. Above is a photograph from Hill's election victory. From left to right are Beresenia Hill, Olivia Hill, Oliver Hill, unidentified, Evalyn Shaed, Lillian Brown, and Dr. Felix Brown. Visiting Farmville and talking to protest leaders Barbara Johns and Leslie Griffin, Hill and Robinson took the case, *Davis v. Prince Edward County*, which was consolidated with four other cases as *Brown v. the Board of Education*. Below are, from left to right, unidentified, Spottswood Robinson, Martin A. Martin, and Oliver Hill Sr. (Above, Oliver White Hill Jr.; below, VUU.)

RICHMOND CRUSADE FOR VOTERS. Disfranchisement was one of the pillars of the Byrd Machine's grip on power. To combat this, Dr. William S. Thornton (above, back row, second from right) called a meeting at Greater Mount Moriah Baptist Church in 1956. There, he joined Dr. William Ferguson Reid (back row, second from left) and John Mitchell Brooks (first row, third from right) to form the Richmond Crusade for Voters, which was dedicated to increasing the black vote through voter education and registration drives and endorsing candidates for office. It proved a potent political force in Richmond. Its first major triumph was the 1967 election of Dr. Reid (below) as the first African American member of the Virginia House of Delegates since Reconstruction. (Above, VCU; below, Brenda Hill.)

THALHIMERS IN DOWNTOWN RICHMOND. All through the 1950s and 1960s, downtown Richmond was the place to shop, eat, socialize, take the children to see Santa Claus and the Easter Bunny, and watch the latest movies. Anchoring the impressive shopping blocks between Adams and Tenth Streets were the two largest department stores, Thalhimers and Miller & Rhoads. In 1842, William Thalhimer, a German-Jewish immigrant, established a dry goods store in Richmond. At its height of popularity, 1945–1980, the Thalhimers store grew to six stories. Its Richmond Room restaurant and lunch counter were the sites of the 1960 arrests. In 1992, the downtown store shut down, and the building was razed in 2004. (Both, VHC.)

MILLER & RHOADS IN DOWNTOWN RICHMOND. Miller & Rhoads, Thalhimers's leading rival, was likewise founded in Richmond as a dry goods establishment—in 1885 by Webster Rhoads, Linton Miller, and Simon Gerhart. Gerhart's name was dropped after he moved to Lynchburg. As with Thalhimers, its heyday was during the 1950s to 1970s. The store became particularly noted for its Santaland every Christmas season with its legendary Santa Claus. Its English Tea Room restaurant was as renowned as Thalhimers's Richmond Room and followed the same segregation policy—thus, it was one of the targets of the 1960 sit-in. After years of decline, the downtown store closed its doors in 1990, and the old Miller & Rhoads building was occupied by a Hilton hotel. (Both, LOV.)

CIVIL WAR CENTENNIAL AND THALHIMERS EXHIBIT. As the 100th anniversary of the Civil War approached, there was a spate of commemorations, exhibits, and events all around Virginia and in Richmond in particular. The ethos was strongly pro-Confederate. The building that housed the main exhibitions was later altered and converted to Larrick Hall, a building of the Virginia Commonwealth University campus now serving as a student center. At Thalhimers Department Store, one of the window displays exhibited busts of Confederate figures like Robert E. Lee and Stonewall Jackson. (Above, LOV; below, VHC.)

Two

VIRGINIA UNION UNIVERSITY, TO 1960

In 1865, two educational institutions founded by the American Baptist Home Mission Society (ABHMS) commenced operations. Both were established for the purpose of providing learning opportunities for former slaves in the aftermath of emancipation: one was Wayland College & Seminary in Washington, DC, and the other was Richmond Theological School for Freedmen, which, ironically, rented its first campus at the former Lumpkin's Slave Jail in Richmond.

In the 1890s, the ABHMS purchased acreage on Lombardy Street in what was then Henrico County, and on February 11, 1899, representatives from the two institutions met on the new campus to merge them into a comprehensive university, aptly named Virginia Union University. Nine buildings were constructed with Virginia granite and Georgia pine. Architect John Hopper Coxhead directed the construction. The university focused on the education of African American students within a rigidly segregated society, waging an uphill struggle against discrimination. A significant development occurred in 1932 when the neighboring African American women's institution, Hartshorn Memorial College, merged with the previously all-male university, and the campus became coeducational.

The university thrived and, closely connected to Jackson Ward, educated generations of teachers, lawyers, ministers, entrepreneurs, scientists, social activists, journalists, and artists.

In 1960, the president of the university was Dr. Samuel Dewitt Proctor, who had earlier shown his mettle in calmly dealing with a white supremacist threat. The Ku Klux Klan had erected a cross on campus, and Dr. Proctor informed the police, took a photograph, dismantled the cross, and announced that class schedules would proceed without disruption. Dr. Proctor was a close friend of Dr. Martin Luther King Jr., who visited the Virginia Union campus and instructed a new generation of students on nonviolence. It was this generation, born in the 1940s and coming of age in the 1960s, who would soon take up the challenge and make their statement against the Byrd regime.

LUMPKIN'S JAIL.

ORIGINAL CAMPUS OF RICHMOND THEOLOGICAL SCHOOL FOR FREEDMEN. There has never been a more ironic foundation site for a historically black university than this one, the largest slave auctioneering establishment in Richmond. Located in the Shockoe Bottom district around Franklin and Fifteenth Streets, it was owned by Robert Lumpkin and was known as the "Devil's Half Acre" because of the brutality that occurred on its premises. Lumpkin freed and married one of his own slaves who, as Mary F. Lumpkin, inherited the property when Lumpkin died in 1866. The building depicted here served as the actual holding facility where slaves were imprisoned pending their sale. A meeting between Mary Lumpkin and the abolitionist Dr. Nathaniel Colver outside of First African Baptist Church led to the renting of the complex as the school's first campus. (VUU.)

Philª June 28ᵗʰ /69

Mr Corey
Dear Sir,
I received your letter and was pleased to hear of your safe arrival in Boston, and that you were pleased with your visit to the Jubilee. I have never received any letter or papers here from no one, for you, since you left. Mr Gladmum was here to see me about a week ago, was quite well, and pleased to know that you stopped with me He is still anxious about his money and expects to return to Richmond in July. I received a letter from Mr Davis and he says every body is pressing for settlements and I wrote to Dr. Peck to see if he could advance me some money on the property if they were not disposed to buy it is impossible to get any in Richmond and you would oblige me very much if you would

Letter from Mary F. Lumpkin to Dr. Charles Henry Corey. No known image exists of Mary F. Lumpkin; the sole description of her states that she was a "large, fair faced woman." She is variously referred to as "Mary Anne," "Mary Jane," or "Mary F. Lumpkin," which is how she signed her name. She is known to have had five children by Lumpkin and, according to the account of the incarcerated fugitive slave Anthony Burns, she secretly comforted him by sneaking him a Bible during his imprisonment at Lumpkin's. After selling the Lumpkin complex, Mary Lumpkin moved to New Orleans, and then to Richmond, Ohio, where she passed away in 1905. The "Holmes" and "Jones" she refers to in this letter are Pastor James Henry Holmes and Dr. Joseph Endom Jones Sr. (VUU.)

Dr. Nathaniel Colver and Dr. Charles Henry Corey. Dr. Nathaniel Colver (1794–1870) labored for most of his life as a minister and abolitionist. After the war, he spearheaded efforts by the American Baptist Home Mission Society to establish a school in the South for training former slaves for the ministry. He finalized the campus rental with Mary Lumpkin and taught at the school for a year before retiring because of ill health. His place was taken by Dr. Charles Henry Corey (1834–1899), who directed the institution (renamed Richmond Theological Seminary in 1886) for 30 years before it merged with Wayland Seminary in 1899 to form Virginia Union University. (Both, VUU.)

PASTOR JAMES HENRY HOLMES (1826–1900). James Henry Holmes was born on a slave plantation in King and Queen County, Virginia, but was hired out by his master to work in a Richmond tobacco factory. Arrested in 1848 for helping his father-in-law escape on the Underground Railroad, Holmes was sold and sent to New Orleans, where he nearly died during a steamship boiler explosion. In 1855, he was sold to another master, who moved to Richmond. Holmes rejoined the congregation of First African Baptist Church, where he was elected pastor in 1867. He and his family lived for a while at the Lumpkin Jail site and were instrumental in establishing Richmond Theological School for Freedmen. In 1878, he became one of the school's first African American trustees and served in that capacity until October 1900. He was noted for his firm stance against racism and his encouragement of the young Maggie Lena Walker, who was one of his parishioners. (VUU.)

Dr. Jones (1852–1922). From Lynchburg, Virginia, Joseph Endom Jones was among the first students at Richmond Theological School for Freedmen, attending from 1868 to 1871. He was born into slavery but rapidly advanced after he secured his freedom, ultimately earning a master's degree from Colgate University and a doctor of divinity from Selma University. He taught homiletics and philosophy at Virginia Union University for 46 years, from 1876 to 1922. Jones focused on developing leadership skills and a sense of social justice in his students, a quality he also imparted to his son Eugene Kinckle Jones Sr., who became one of the founders ("jewels") of Alpha Phi Alpha Fraternity in 1906 while at Cornell University; he was also secretary to the Urban League and a member of Pres. Franklin D. Roosevelt's "Black Cabinet." (VUU.)

Dr. MacVicar (1829–1904). Dr. Malcolm MacVicar, from Argyleshire, Scotland, was a veteran preacher and professor at churches and educational institutions in diverse locations in the United States and Canada. A tough and determined man whose grandfatherly demeanor belied his strength of will, he battled racial discrimination with biting sarcasm and was not afraid to go head to head with the powers that be. A secretary of the American Baptist Home Mission Society, he was more than any other individual responsible for engineering the merger of Wayland Seminary and Richmond Theological Seminary to forge Virginia Union University in 1899. At the age of 70, he became the fledgling institution's first president. His administration set the tone for high academic standards, self-discipline, and a feisty refusal to countenance injustice. He passed away on commencement day, May 17, 1904. (VUU.)

VIRGINIA UNION CAMPUS PANORAMIC VIEW (C. 1907). The ground-breaking for construction on the campus of the new Virginia Union University at 1500 North Lombardy Street occurred on February 11, 1899, and on October 4, 1899, classes began. In all, nine structures (later dubbed the "Nine Noble Buildings") were completed. From left to right are the power plant (with smokestack),

the barn, Industrial Hall, Kingsley Hall (the dormitory), Pickford Hall (the principal administrative and classroom building), Baptist Memorial Hall (the original dean's residence), Coburn Hall (the chapel and library), Porter Cottage (the original president's residence), and Martin E. Gray Hall (the cafeteria). (LOC.)

VIRGINIA UNION UNIVERSITY: MARTIN E. GRAY HALL. One of the "Nine Noble Buildings" that were initially set on the campus for Virginia Union University from 1899 to 1900, Martin E. Gray Hall was, like the others, constructed of Virginia granite with inlaid interior Georgia pine. The buildings were designed in the then popular Victorian Romanesque style by architect John Hopper Coxhead (1863–1943), from Buffalo, New York. Designated as the dining hall, this structure was named for Martin E. Gray of Willoughby, Ohio, who owned a large farm there and had donated $25,000 to assure the school's construction. Coxhead, who personally oversaw the construction of all the buildings, was adamant that the students themselves physically participated in the actual process. Martin E. Gray Hall was to play a crucial role as a focal point during the event of February 1960. (VUU.)

Dr. Lyman Beecher Tefft (1833–1926). Born in Exeter, Rhode Island, Tefft was an active abolitionist minister affiliated with the American Baptist Home Missionary Society. Obtaining a doctorate in divinity from Brown University, Dr. Tefft was appointed principal of Nashville Normal and Theological Institute in 1873, an HBCU that specialized in training African American men for the ministry and women for the teaching profession. In 1883, he conceived, helped establish, and served for 29 years as the first president of Hartshorn Memorial College, an institution catering exclusively to African American women, on the corner of Lombardy and Leigh Streets in Richmond. The curriculum was based on that of Wellesley College, and Tefft's conception of women's education was very advanced for its time, inculcating in the students the idea of preparation for assuming leadership or partnership roles with men rather than subordination. (VUU.)

CARRIE VICTORIA DYER (1839–1921). Dr. Tefft's partner in the establishment and day-to-day running of Hartshorn Memorial College was Carrie Victoria Dyer, who served as college principal and later dean. She was a native of Constantine, Michigan, but moved to the South after the Civil War, first to Nashville, where she met and collaborated with Dr. Tefft at Nashville Normal and Theological Institute, then to Richmond. She acted as a role model for her students and functioned as the college's chief fundraiser and correspondent. Like Dr. Tefft, she was an adamant proponent of single-gender education over the coeducational model. Dr. Tefft retired in 1912, and Dyer was named college dean. In 1914, she relinquished the deanship and taught classes at Hartshorn for one more year before retiring. Shortly thereafter, Hartshorn went into decline. (VUU.)

DR. TEFFT WITH THE HARTSHORN CLASS OF 1899. Dr. Tefft envisioned the women who graduated from Hartshorn to be strong moral role models for their husbands, families, and students and capable of holding their own intellectually. Eva Roberta Coles (seated, second from left) would soon gain renown as a Christian missionary to the Congo. Hartshorn became well known throughout the South for its excellence in teacher training and as a scourge to Richmond saloon owners for its strong support of the temperance movement. Though Dr. Tefft was an opponent of coeducational instruction, his insistence on the worth and equality of female students influenced neighboring Virginia Union University, which had previously been all male, to adopt the coeducational model in 1928. Hartshorn Memorial merged into Virginia Union in 1932, importing into the university its tradition of self-reliant and confident women, unafraid to challenge the established order. (VUU.)

DR. RAYFORD WHITTINGHAM LOGAN (1897–1982). Dr. Logan, who earned his doctorate at Harvard University in 1936, stands among the most distinguished African American historians of the early 20th century and strongly influenced activist Dr. Tinsley L. Spraggins, who would figure in the events of February 1960. He taught at Virginia Union University from 1925 to 1930, serving as chair of the history department and gaining notice for his fiery and erudite lectures condemning colonialism and racism. His vehemence got him into difficulties with the university administration and his appointment was discontinued, despite student protests. He served in Pres. Franklin D. Roosevelt's "Black Cabinet" and continued his academic career as a history professor at Howard University from 1938 to 1965. His books (both published in 1954) include *The Betrayal of the Negro* and *The Negro in American Life and Thought: The Nadir, 1877–1901*. (VUU.)

Dr. John Malcus Ellison (1889–1979). Dr. Ellison was the first African American and alumnus to become president of Virginia Union University. Attending VUU from 1909 to 1917 and matriculating with a bachelor of arts in sociology, Ellison capped his education with a doctorate in Christian education and sociology from Drew University in 1933. The crucial accomplishment of his long administration (1941–1955) was the establishment of the graduate School of Theology. His fundraising skills enabled the university to transport the landmark Belgian Friendship building from New York to the campus. The leaders who came out of this school would play a significant role in the years ahead and would include Presidents Samuel Dewitt Proctor, Allix James, and David Shannon as well as Frank Pinkston, Charles Sherrod, Edward McCreary, Curtis Harris, Ralph Reavis, Bishop Leontine Kelly, Jeremiah Wright, Miles Jerome Jones, and Wyatt Tee Walker. (VUU.)

ALICE CARLOTTA JACKSON STUART (1913–2001). The first of the Virginia Union women to challenge the Jim Crow system in Virginia, Stuart first attended Hartshorn, then Virginia Union, graduating with an English degree in 1934. In 1935, she applied for admission to the University of Virginia graduate school to study for a master's degree in French but was turned down because of race. The ensuing protest led to the NAACP, under Dr. J.M. Tinsley, threatening to take the university to court. Legal action was avoided when Stuart accepted a scholarship from the State of Virginia to study French at Columbia University. She earned her master's degree there in 1937 and embarked on a teaching career. Her action forced the Virginia General Assembly to authorize the first graduate school for African Americans—at Virginia State College. (VUU.)

JANET JONES BALLARD (1930–1996) AND RUBY CLAYTON WALKER (1938–2014). The foundation upon which the Richmond 34 staged their protest was laid by the activities of individual activists. Two such precursors were Janet Jones Ballard and Ruby Clayton Walker. Ballard, a Virginia Union and Virginia State graduate who became the international president of Alpha Kappa Alpha sorority, refused to tolerate segregation laws in downtown Richmond. Her tenacity forced Thalhimers to integrate its beauty salon even prior to 1960. On December 16, 2017, she was honored by a monument stone at Virginia Union. Both she and Walker participated in the Campaign for Human Dignity. Walker, a longtime social worker at the Richmond Social Services Bureau, was also in the forefront of the opposition to the closure of Prince Edward County Schools. (Above, Dr. Kimberly A. Matthews; right, VUU.)

DR. WYATT TEE WALKER AND THE MOSQUE. On January 1, 1959, the pastor of Gillfield Baptist Church in Petersburg, Virginia, Dr. Wyatt Tee Walker, held a prayer pilgrimage at the Mosque Auditorium protesting "Massive Resistance". This was to be followed by a 17-block march through Richmond. Expecting attendance of perhaps 500 in severe weather, he was amazed by a turnout that numbered at least three times that. Dr. Martin Luther King Jr. wrote to Walker: "Virginia and the Nation will be in your debt for many years to come." The Mosque, built in 1927 by members of the Acca Temple Shrine, was renamed the Landmark Theater in 1995 and then the Altria Theater in 2014. Dr. King himself spoke there at the Second Pilgrimage of Prayer on January 1, 1960. (Left, VUU; below, DHR.)

Three

The "Oil" on the "Flame," February 1–22, 1960

The Greensboro sit-in on February 1, 1960, ignited a series of nonviolent protests that began to sweep through the Southern border states. On Saturday, February 20, 1960, two graduate theological students from Virginia Union University, Frank George Pinkston and Charles Melvin Sherrod, assembled some 200 students at the Martin E. Gray Hall on campus. They marched from campus to the downtown shopping district to occupy seats at the lunch counters. But, as it was a Saturday, the stores simply closed.

On Monday, February 22, 1960, three hundred students assembled on the Virginia Union campus as before, marched downtown, and staged sit-ins at the whites-only lunch counters of Woolworth, Grant, and Murphy department stores, Peoples' drug stores, Miller & Rhoads tearoom, and the Thalhimers lunch counter/soda fountain and Richmond Room restaurant. At Thalhimers, the store management threatened the students with arrest, and while some got up, 34 remained. When they refused to move, the management had the police arrest them. They were verbally abused by some of the white customers, and at least one woman had hot coffee deliberately spilled on her. NAACP attorneys Oliver Hill, Clarence Newsome, and Martin A. Martin were on the scene even as the students were being arrested. As he was being led to the wagon, Pinkston announced to crowds milling around outside: "The students have set the flame. Now we challenge you to put some oil on it and keep a blaze going." Some students were as young as 18; most no older than 23. The oldest was 48. Those arrested were herded into six patrol wagons, and by the time they reached the prison, a crowd of 500 was waiting, some carrying American flags and cheering the students. The bail money was quickly raised, and upon release, the 34 were triumphantly feted at the Hotel Eggleston on Second and Leigh Streets.

Dr. Samuel DeWitt Proctor (1921–1997). Born in Norfolk, Samuel DeWitt Proctor attended Virginia State College but left and enrolled at Virginia Union University to pursue a career in the ministry, graduating with a bachelor's degree in 1942. After a year's study at the University of Pennsylvania, Proctor pursued religious studies at Crozer Theological Seminary, where he earned his bachelor's degree in divinity in 1945. After another year at Yale University, Proctor entered the Boston University School of Theology and earned a doctorate in 1950. His former mentor at Virginia Union University, Pres. John Malcus Ellison, brought him back as a teacher and administrator, and he succeeded Ellison as university president in 1955. As one of the nation's youngest university presidents and a skilled fundraiser, he pulled Virginia Union out of a $90,000 shortfall. Steeped in the activist theology of Reinhold Niehbuhr, he quietly encouraged students in nonviolence against racism. (VUU.)

DINING ROOM AT MARTIN E. GRAY HALL. Many photographs exist of the Martin E. Gray building, but there are few of the actual dining hall. It functioned as a rallying point for 200–300 Virginia Union students assembling there on February 20 and 22, 1960, to organize their protest. Sadly, the interior, which was beautifully inlaid with Georgia pine, was gutted by a devastating fire in 1993. The granite walls proved indestructible, and it was fortunate that the university administration had taken an insurance policy that paid for all but $50,000 of the damage; the building was repaired and functional within less than two years. It now houses the offices and classrooms for the Evelyn Syphax School of Education. Because of its role as the starting point for protest, a Richmond 34 monument stone was placed in front of Martin E. Gray Hall in 2010. (VUU.)

Dr. Martin Luther King Jr. on the Virginia Union Campus. Dr. King and Dr. Samuel DeWitt Proctor enjoyed a long-standing friendship. They met in 1950 when Proctor was giving a lecture at Crozer Theological Seminary, where King was a student. Proctor became a mentor for Dr. King, and Proctor's appointment as VUU president almost coincided with King's assuming the pastorate of Dexter Avenue Baptist Church in Montgomery, Alabama, just as the Montgomery bus boycott crisis exploded. During the tense months of the boycott, stretching into 1956, Proctor was often King's guest and through his sermons and lectures would offer vital support. In return, King visited the Richmond campus on many occasions to tutor the students in the principles of nonviolence. This photograph shows King's last visit to VUU. King, at left, is addressing a reporter; Coretta Scott King is at far right. Dr. Thomas Henderson is third from left at the back, followed by Senators Jacob Javits and Paul Douglas, and Dr. Ralph Abernathy. (VUU.)

STUDENT PROTEST MARCH DOWN LOMBARDY STREET, FEBRUARY 20, 1960. The first sit-in in downtown Richmond occurred on Saturday, February 20, 1960. On the front page of the *Richmond Afro-American* was "BULLETIN: Virginia Union University students in Richmond indicated this week that they are fully in accord with the trend of the widely-spreading lunch counter demonstrations." Assembling on campus, 200 students filed onto Lombardy Street and walked north, where these photographs were taken near a railroad underpass, since demolished. At Broad Street, they turned right to the main shopping area where they stationed themselves in segregated seats at the department stores. Since it was Saturday, the store managers simply closed early. The first day of the sit-in passed mainly without incident. It would be different two days later. (Both, UVA.)

Sit-ins at Murphy's and Woolworth's. On Monday, February 22, 1960, the Virginia Union students—this time estimated to number around 300—converged upon the downtown shopping district. Since this was a major sales day, George Washington's birthday, early closing was not an option, and the students occupied every seat they could. Scenes like these took place at F.W. Woolworth's (above) and J.C. Murphy's (below) on Broad Street near Thalhimers and Miller & Rhoads. The students were uniformly quiet, well-attired, and orderly, and most brought textbooks and study materials with them. (Above, VUU; below, Malcolm O. Carpenter photograph, Prints & Photographs Division, LOC.)

THALHIMERS, FEBRUARY 22, 1960. William Blum Thalhimer Jr. (1914–2005), pictured above at center, was the fourth generation in his family who conducted retail trade in Richmond, and in 1950, he had become company president and general manager. At the time of the sit-in, shopping malls were few and had not yet caught on, and the downtown store generated most of the company's business. The renowned Richmond Room restaurant was a focus for the student protestors. Thalhimers became fully integrated in January 1961, the first of Richmond's major retailers to do so. Thalhimer retired as CEO in 1984. (Above, RTD; below, VHC.)

> We point out to you that this is the private property of Thalhimer Brothers, Incorporated. We request you to leave the premises. Your refusal to leave constitutes a trespass which is a misdemeanor upon conviction of which you may be fined up to one hundred dollars or confined in jail up to thirty days or both.

THALHIMERS WARNING CARD AND PINKSTON AND HAMBLETT. While the students were occupying seats at the lunch counter and in the Richmond Room, they were handed cards by Thalhimers management indicating that they were trespassing on the company's property and that a refusal to leave could be cause for their arrest, with possible consequences of fines and/or imprisonment. The card pictured here was given to Raymond B. Randolph Jr., protest leader. Frank George Pinkston is shown below in discussion with Thalhimer vice president Newman Hamblett prior to his own arrest. (Above, Raymond B. Randolph Jr.; below, VHC.)

THE ARREST OF LEROY M. BRAY JR., FEBRUARY 22, 1960. The first to be arrested of 34 Virginia Union University students for attempting to integrate the dining facilities at Thalhimers, Leroy M. Bray Jr. later confided that, despite the outward display of bravado in this photograph, as he was about to step into the police van, "wheels started spinning" in his mind as he realized that he was actually going to be incarcerated. He was more anxious then about what his parents might think rather than about what might lie in store for him at the jail, a worry shared by many of his Richmond 34 colleagues. According to Bray, he became the first in line by happenstance when others in front of him moved when confronted by the Thalhimer manager's ultimatum. (VHC.)

CHARLES M. SHERROD. Charles Melvin Sherrod was born in Surry County, Virginia. He enrolled at Virginia Union and graduated with a bachelor of arts degree in 1958. At the time of the Richmond sit-in, he was studying toward a bachelor's degree in divinity, which he would complete in 1961. Along with Frank Pinkston and Woodrow Grant, he served as one of the principal leaders of the student protest who had prior meetings with Dr. Samuel DeWitt Proctor. As a protest director, he notably maintained a firm discipline and defused a potentially explosive situation on at least one occasion. After his arrest and release on bail, Sherrod attended the Shaw University Conference on April 14–15, 1960, and, with Pinkston, Elizabeth Johnson, Laura Greene, and Virginius Bray Thornton III, became a charter member of the Student Nonviolent Coordinating Committee (SNCC). (VUU.)

Frank George Pinkston Sr. Taken to Jail. At the time of his arrest as one of the leaders and organizers of the Richmond sit-in, Frank George Pinkston Sr. was working on his master's degree in theology at Virginia Union. Born on May 20, 1936, in Silver Springs, Florida, Pinkston entered Virginia Union in 1953 and graduated with a bachelor's degree in English in 1958. Enrolling in the School of Theology graduate program, he finished in 1961, also serving as assistant football coach under the tutelage of legendary head coach "Tricky Tom" Harris. Like Sherrod, a charter member of SNCC, Pinkston taught English at Howard High School in Ocala, Florida, and in 1963, as chair of the Marion County branch of the NAACP, organized and led a countywide civil rights campaign. He is still known there as the "Black Liberator of Marion County." A portion of US Highway 27 was named after him. In 1973, he succumbed to a heart attack in Sioux Falls, South Dakota. (UVA.)

OUTSIDE THE JAIL AND THE EGGLESTON HOTEL. The city jail was a block away from Thalhimers, near the old Marshall Street Farmer's Market (left background). Richmond police, employing German shepherd dogs, held back the crowds. The students were released after being charged, fingerprinted, and incarcerated for a short time before their bonds were paid. The 34 were then escorted in vehicles to the Eggleston Hotel at Second and Leigh Streets, where they were hailed as heroes. The Eggleston had been one of the significant centers for Richmond's Jackson Ward district and had counted as its guests noted figures of the Harlem Renaissance. (Above, RTD; left, DHR.)

THE ARREST OF RUTH NELSON TINSLEY. The most disturbing image of the Richmond sit-in occurred one day later, on February 23, 1960: the arrest of 59-year-old Ruth Nelson Tinsley (1900–1970), the wife of NAACP director Dr. Jesse Tinsley, who was picketing outside Thalhimers. A police officer ordered her to move and when she refused, he carried her, with the help of another officer, across Broad Street to the police station. The story made national news, and photographs of her arrest appeared in the March 7, 1960, issue of *Life* magazine. (Both, Malcolm O. Carpenter, Prints and Photograph Division, LOC.)

DR. FRANKLIN JOHNSON GAYLES AND "TRICKY TOM" HARRIS. There was no lack of inspirational figures at Virginia Union for the Richmond 34 and others to emulate. Dr. Franklin Johnson Gayles (1920–2013, left) taught political science there for 33 years and constantly encouraged the students in their political activism. Practicing what he preached, he was elected Richmond's first African American city treasurer in 1977 and served until 1992. Coach Thomas "Tricky Tom" Harris (below), who was VUU athletic director from 1950 to 1982, instilled a sense of self-esteem and competitiveness in his students. One of his assistant football coaches was Frank George Pinkston. (Both, VUU.)

ELIZABETH J. JOHNSON AND TINSLEY L. SPRAGGINS. In later years, Richmond 34 members and other Virginia Union students of the day would cite some of their professors as role models. Among the two most often cited are Elizabeth Jones Johnson and Tinsley L. Spraggins. Johnson, who taught commerce, was also the mother of two of the 34 students arrested: Elizabeth Patricia Johnson and Ford T. Johnson Jr. In 1969, she became the first African American assistant dean of admissions at the University of Virginia. Dr. Tinsley L. Spraggins, who taught history, played a role in coaching leaders of the sit-in and was the most activist member of the university faculty during the 1960s. (Both, VUU.)

Dr. David Thomas Shannon (1933–2008). David Shannon was a prodigy who became a minister at the age of 16. Having earned bachelor of art and bachelor of divinity degrees at Virginia Union University, he secured a master's degree in divinity at the Oberlin Graduate School of Theology, a PhD from the University of Pittsburgh, and a doctorate in divinity from Vanderbilt University. In 1960, he was on the faculty of Virginia Union and pastor at Ebenezer Baptist Church. A staunch supporter of Dr. King and Dr. Proctor, he was active in the background, fostering student activism. As one of the university's best-liked and most skillful and articulate instructors, he was chosen, along with Dr. Edward D. McCreary and Dr. Tinsley Spraggins, to calm the student demonstrators in the aftermath of the arrest of the Richmond 34 and urge them to return to campus. Dr. Shannon later served as dean of the Pittsburgh Theological Seminary and eighth president of Virginia Union University, from 1979 to 1985. (VUU.)

Dr. Edward D. McCreary Jr. and Dean Wendell Phillips Russell. At least four Virginia Union University faculty members were at the scene as the 34 students were arrested and were trusted enough by the student body to persuade them to call off the protest and return to classes. Besides Dr. Spraggins and Dr. Shannon, they were Dr. Edward D. McCreary Jr. (1919–2014) and Dr. Wendell Phillips Russell (1926–1991). Dr. McCreary was fond of relating how his father had walked all the way from Alabama in order to study at Virginia Union and he himself served as a professor in the Department of Religion and Philosophy there for 39 years. The dean of students at Virginia Union in 1960, Dr. Russell later served as the eighth president of Virginia State University (1970–1974). (Both, VUU.)

WOODROW BENJAMIN GRANT JR. BEING LED TO JAIL. What was quite remarkable about the 1960 Richmond sit-in, in comparison to other civil rights protests, was that, for the most part, all went in a very orderly fashion, and as with Woodrow Benjamin Grant Jr., the students were neatly, even formally, dressed and marched purposefully alongside the officers. Two of the women students later recounted that they had been spat upon, and Elizabeth Patricia Johnson was deliberately scalded by hot coffee. Racial epithets were of course heard from some in the crowd, and some white men did show up at Thalhimers waving Confederate flags, but they were blocked by police. Reports on police behavior were mixed: Gloria Collins related that an officer was polite and even helped her into the wagon; Marise Ellison stated that they were very rude and surly. (UVA.)

Dr. Allix Bledsoe James (1922–2015). Dr. James was the dean of the Virginia Union School of Theology at the time of the Richmond sit-in. When he heard of the arrest of the Richmond 34 students, he and his wife, Susan Nickens James, offered their house as collateral to raise some of the bail money. A native of Marshall, Texas, James studied for his bachelor's at Virginia Union and completed his studies at Richmond's Union Theological Seminary, where he was invested with a doctor of theology degree in 1957. In 1947, he joined Virginia Union's faculty and rose through the administrative ranks from dean of students (1950–1956), dean of the School of Theology (1956–1960), vice president (1960–1970), and seventh VUU president (1970–1979). Among the major accomplishments of his administration was the creation of the Sydney Lewis School of Business. The rebuilt chapel on campus is named in his honor. (VUU.)

Dr. LaVerne Charmayne Byrd Smith (1927–2017). The third contributor to raising the bail money for the Richmond 34 was the VUU alumnae chapter of Alpha Kappa Alpha sorority, under its formidable basileus (president) Dr. Laverne Charmayne Byrd Smith. The chapter cancelled its annual ball and used the funds set aside for it to secure the students' release. Dr. Smith was an imposing figure who believed in directly and unflinchingly combatting racism. In 1948, she received a bachelor of arts degree in history/education from Virginia Union University and proceeded in 1964 to attain a master's degree in educational psychology and reading from Virginia State College and in 1985 a doctorate in education, curriculum, and instruction from the University of Maryland. From 1944 to 1990, she was involved as teacher, mentor, and administrator (including state supervisor of reading and language development) in Virginia's public schools and at Virginia Union. She was the author of *Traveling on . . .*, a two-volume history of First Baptist Church of South Richmond, and several works of poetry. (VUU.)

EDWARD H. PEEPLES. Dr. Edward H. Peeples was the only white person to participate in solidarity with the protestors. On February 20, 1960, at Thalhimer, store manager Newman Hamblett ordered Peeples from the store, and two men took him out, not too gently, and threw him onto the sidewalk, telling him never to return. Peeples had graduated in 1957 from Richmond Professional Institute (now Virginia Commonwealth University) and returned in 1963 to teach at his alma mater. He held the title of associate professor emeritus there, having earned his doctorate in philosophy from the University of Kentucky in 1972. He had a long career as a civil rights activist, as recounted in his autobiography *Scalawag: A White Southerner's Journey through Segregation to Human Rights Activism*. (Dr. Edward H. Peeples.)

FIFTH STREET BAPTIST CHURCH. Through the worst years of the nadir in race relations, the black churches, in conjunction with black colleges and schools and black fraternal organizations, were the main pillars nurturing and sustaining the African American urban communities. After the arrest of the 34, a mass meeting at Fifth Street Baptist Church launched the Campaign for Human Dignity and hastened the end of segregation in Richmond. The church was founded in 1880. Its pastor in 1960, Dr. Christopher Columbus Scott, served for years on the executive committee of the Richmond branch of the NAACP, working in tandem with Dr. Jesse Tinsley, and had been an active supporter of the electoral campaigns of attorney Oliver Hill, who was the featured speaker at the meeting. Hill gave an impassioned speech to a crowd of some 3,000, and the massive boycott started in earnest. (Dr. Kimberly A. Matthews.)

Four

THE CAMPAIGN FOR HUMAN DIGNITY, 1960–1963

After the Richmond 34 arrests, the Richmond Citizen's Advisory Committee (RCAC) formed under the chairmanship of Rev. P.B. Walker. Protests and picketing continued on a daily basis and expanded to other establishments and areas of the city—Peoples' drug stores; McCargo-Baldwin on Hull Street; King's drive-in restaurant and The Ranch, both on Lombardy Street; the White Tower chain; and all segregated movie theaters. VUU students and the RCAC combined to launch the Campaign for Human Dignity, which included an economic boycott of businesses that practiced discrimination.

The Virginia Union students attending the Shaw University Conference of April 14–15, 1960, organized by Ella Baker, who launched SNCC, were Pinkston, Sherrod, Elizabeth Johnson, Virginius Thornton Bray III, and Laura Greene. They returned to an on-campus public meeting at the Belgian Friendship Building, where they mapped out the new strategy for social activism in central Virginia. High school students were enlisted to participate in the cause and were introduced to nonviolent resistance techniques.

Even during the summer, some 300 VUU students continued the protests under the direction of a steering committee chaired by Rev. Cleveland Williams and assisted by Sandra Reese, Laura Greene, Frances Barcroft, Obadiah Simms, and Woodrow B. Grant.

By Christmas 1960, the downtown merchants began to feel the sting of the RCAC's campaign. Thalhimers alone saw a 3.9 percent drop in sales for 1960, the company's worst year to date. By February 1961, Thalhimers and most businesses began implementing desegregation. The campaign had succeeded. The 34 stood trial and were convicted and assessed a $20 trespassing fine. The verdict was appealed by lawyers Martin A. Martin and Clarence Newsome and the case went before the US Supreme Court as *Raymond B. Randolph, Jr., et al. v. the Commonwealth of Virginia*. On June 10, 1963, the court overturned the convictions.

PICKETS/BOYCOTTING. Nonviolent protest broke out all around Richmond and took various forms, but centered on the urban downtown area. Some carried signs reading "Don't Buy Where You May Be Arrested," "Turn In Your Charge-A-Plate," "Khrushchev Can Eat Here, We Can't," and "Can't Eat . . . Don't Buy." Under the unrelenting pressure of drastically dropping sales figures and adverse publicity, the department stores, bus stations, and assorted smaller shops and restaurants bowed to the laws of economics and gradually implemented desegregation in both the serving of customers and the hiring of employees. (Above, Malcolm O. Carpenter photograph, Prints & Photographs Division, LOC; below, VHC.)

FORD TUCKER JOHNSON JR. The younger brother of Elizabeth Patricia Johnson, Ford Tucker Johnson Jr. formed half of the only pair of siblings arrested on February 22, 1960. He was soon to wage his own struggle against racism in Virginia. While driving with expired license tags, he was pulled over by police and summoned to appear in traffic court. (He was unaware at the time that new license tags were in the car.) Coming to court on April 27, 1962, he inadvertently sat in a section that the presiding judge, Herman A. Cooper, had designated as reserved for whites. Told first by the bailiff and then by the judge to move to the "colored" section, Johnson stayed where he was and was charged with contempt of court. His conviction for contempt was appealed and went before the US Supreme Court as *Ford T. Johnson Jr. vs. Virginia*. On April 29, 1963, the court overturned Johnson's conviction, declaring, "A state may not require segregation in a courtroom." (VUU.)

MARTIN A. MARTIN AND CLARENCE W. NEWSOME. Martin Armstrong Martin (1910–1963) was a graduate of Howard University Law School. He joined with Oliver Hill and Spottswood Robinson III to establish the firm of Hill, Martin & Robinson and defended the Martinsville Seven, African Americans charged with raping a white woman. He was present at Thalhimers with lawyer Clarence W. Newsome on February 22, 1960, and offered encouragement to the students, and, in collaboration with Newsome, appealed their trespassing convictions in the case of *Raymond B. Randolph, Jr., et al. v. the Commonwealth of Virginia*. Newsome read a letter from Dr. King to the 34, which commended their actions. The US Supreme Court handed down its decision to overturn the convictions on June 10, 1963. Sadly, both Martin and Newsome died suddenly from heart seizures shortly before the decision was rendered. (Above, LOC; left, the Clarence W. Newsome family.)

REGINALD M. GREEN AND RALPH REAVIS. VUU ministry student Reginald M. Green Sr. and three other students, Willie E. Rucker, Andre B. Smith, and Harry Lee Snead, were arrested on trespassing charges when they sat at the White Tower restaurant counter. Their appeal, *Reginald M. Green et al. v. Virginia*, nullified their conviction on June 22, 1964. Reginald Green later participated in the freedom rides and served as pastor of Walker Memorial Baptist Church for 40 years. In February 1961, Ralph Reavis, the 21-year-old pastor at Promised Land Baptist Church in Bedford County, led a contingent of eight into the segregated premises of Patterson's Drug Store in Lynchburg. While they were arrested and being led away to jail, they defiantly sang "We are Climbing Jacob's Ladder." Dr. Reavis would rise to the presidency of Virginia University at Lynchburg. (Both, VUU.)

NORFOLK SIT-IN. In Norfolk, the sit-in protests began on February 12, 1960, predating those in Richmond. The students were from what was then the Norfolk branch of Virginia State College (now Virginia State University). The Norfolk branch was originally founded on September 18, 1935, as part of Virginia Union University and became Norfolk State University in 1979. These photographs show students at the Woolworth's store lunch counter. Among the 38 protestors were at least three uniformed ROTC students, as seen above. The Norfolk sit-in resulted in no arrests on that day. (Both, *Virginian-Pilot*.)

Dr. Thomas Howard Henderson and Farmville Protests. Dr. Thomas Howard Henderson (above), a 1929 VUU and 1946 University of Chicago graduate, was appointed dean at Virginia Union in 1941 and president in succession to Dr. Proctor in 1960. Dr. Henderson was, along with J. Rupert Picott and Winfred Mundle, part of the RCAC that coordinated the Campaign for Human Dignity and negotiated with William Thalhimer and other business leaders to bring about desegregation. Dr. Henderson accompanied attorneys Oliver Hill and Spottswood Robinson to Farmville in Prince Edward County, Virginia, in 1951 and took a deep interest in the struggle there. Protests, such as the one seen below on Farmville's North Main Street in July 1963, continued in Prince Edward through the 1960s. (Above, VUU; below, VCU.)

WHITE TOWER. Notorious among the business establishments that stubbornly clung to Jim Crow policies were the fast food restaurants of the White Tower chain (dubbed the "Lily White Towers" by protesting VUU students). One of the chain's many Richmond locations was at the corner of Broad and Lombardy Streets, provocatively near the Virginia Union campus. (RTD.)

PEOPLE'S DRUG STORE. Another such establishment was the People's drug store chain, founded in Alexandria, Virginia, in 1905. The stores were full service and included segregated snack bars. By January 1961, the chain had capitulated and integrated its facilities. People's was sold to CVS Health Corporation in 1990, and the name was discontinued in 1994. (LOV.)

PETERSBURG LIBRARY PROTEST. Dr. Wyatt Tee Walker launched what would be dubbed the "Second Siege of Petersburg" on February 27, 1960, when he marched at the head of some 100 Virginia State College and Peabody High School students to stage a sit-in at the Petersburg Public Library. On March 8, 1960, during a return visit to the library, Dr. Walker and 10 others were arrested on trespassing charges. Repeated protests closed the library for long periods until it finally accepted desegregation in November 1960. (Both, RTD.)

ELIZABETH PATRICIA JOHNSON RICE. After her arrest and prior to her graduation from Virginia Union in 1961, Elizabeth Patricia Johnson participated as one of the university representatives at the April 14–15, 1960, Shaw University Conference and became a charter member of the Student Nonviolent Coordinating Committee. She was selected to appear on the *Today* show representing the university, and debated segregationists. She married another VUU alumnus, Rev. Richard M. Rice, and the couple reared two sons. Elizabeth Rice entered a long career as a public schoolteacher and faced the challenging task of being one of the first two African American teachers at the previously all-white Petersburg High School. She later taught biology in Washington, DC. In 2000, a close brush with death from an aortic aneurysm pointed her life in a new direction. (VUU.)

A.J. Franklin and Joanna Hinton. Anderson J. Franklin graduated from Virginia Union in 1961 with a bachelor's degree in sociology and psychology and enjoyed a distinguished academic career. His Richmond 34 classmate, Joanna Hinton (below), was part of the Virginia Union class of 1962 and participated in the Baptist Student Movement. Franklin studied at Howard University for his master of science degree in experimental psychology (1964), and in 1968, he earned a PhD in counseling psychology at the University of Oregon. Dr. Franklin taught at the City University of New York from 1975 to 2007 and rose to the rank of full professor. In 2007, he was named to the Honorable David S. Nelson Professional Chair at Boston College. In 2018, however, he received a shocking surprise when his passport application was denied because of his 1960 arrest. (Both, VUU.)

GEORGE WENDALL HARRIS JR. AND MILTON JOHNSON. Among the 34 arrested, both George Wendall Harris Jr. (left) and Milton Johnson (below) were a bit older than the others. Johnson, the oldest at 48, was a military veteran who studied for the ministry and graduated in 1963 with a bachelor's degree in social science education. Harris (1936–2015) graduated from Virginia Union in 1963 with a bachelor's degree in business administration. In 1967, he received his law degree from the North Carolina Central University Law School. From 1985 to 2005, he presided as judge over the 23rd Judicial District of Virginia. (Both, VUU.)

RAYMOND B. RANDOLPH JR. AND CEOTIS L. PRYOR. Raymond B. Randolph Jr.'s civil rights activism continued past 1960. The following year, he took part in the freedom rides and was arrested in Mississippi, spending nearly two months at the brutal Parchman Prison. There, Randolph (right) and other freedom riders were placed in maximum security cells, forced to labor on a chain gang, and were at one point deprived of mattresses and bug screens—for singing. Ceotis Lavigne Pryor (1938–2016) continued his education at Virginia Union and graduated from the School of Theology in 1964. Called to be pastor at the Corinthian Baptist Church of Germantown, Pennsylvania, in 1974, he held that position until his retirement in 2007. (Both, VUU.)

ALBERT VAN GRAVES JR. AND SAMUEL F. SHAW. Albert Van Graves Jr. was from Little Rock, Arkansas. Prior to attending Virginia Union University, where he was a starting player on the 1962 football team, he served in the US Marines. He worked for many years at Richmond juvenile detention homes, and upon retiring stayed active by substitute teaching in Northern Virginia. He passed away on September 20, 2008. Samuel Shaw (below) graduated from VUU in 1962 and attended the 2010 reunion. (Left, Albert Van Graves Jr. family; below, VUU)

VIRGINIA SIMMS GEORGE AND MARISE ELLISON SMITH. Virginia Simms, Marise Ellison, and Patricia Washington were close friends at Virginia Union. Virginia Simms George, originally from Newport News, Virginia, graduated from VUU with a degree in history. Because of her long fingernails, it took so long to fingerprint her at the police station that she was bailed out of jail without even having been placed in a cell. She entered into a long career of teaching, counseling, and community activism. Marise Ellison Smith asserts that she was denied a position with a major airline in 1965 because of her trespassing arrest record for the 1960 sit-in. She served in the Red Cross and as an officer of Women Organized Against Rape. Both women report that they were spat upon the day of their arrest. (Both, VUU.)

BARBARA THORNTON NERO AND VIRGINIUS THORNTON BRAY III. Barbara A. Thornton Nero attended Virginia Randolph High School prior to going to VUU and being arrested at Thalhimers. For Thornton and her family, the impact was painful. After the sit-in, her father's lawn maintenance business suffered drastically. She moved to New York City, where she married Robert V. "Bob" Nero Jr. She earned a bachelor of arts degree from Adelphi University and taught for eight years. Virginius Bray Thornton III (1934–2015), after he helped to found SNCC, earned a doctorate at Penn State University and ended a long teaching career at MassBay Community College in 2014. (Left, VUU; below, Monique Nero.)

WENDELL T. FOSTER JR. AND JOHN J. MCCALL. Wendell T. Foster Jr., who graduated from VUU with a bachelor of science degree in mathematics, taught deprived African American students in Prince Edward County during the "Massive Resistance" school closure. He earned a master of science degree at San Jose State University and taught mathematics for many years at J. Sargent Reynolds Community College. John J. McCall, who earned a bachelor of science degree at Virginia Union in 1961, taught for two years in Sierra Leone as a volunteer with the Peace Corps. He worked for 34 years in US government service, monitoring anti-poverty programs for the Office of Economic Opportunity. He died in 2005, but his wife, Geneva McCall, represented him at Richmond 34 events. (Both, VUU.)

GLORIA COLLINS AND BETTY W. MARTIN (LOIS WHITE). Though Gloria Claudette Collins Grinnell had experienced racism growing up in California, going to Virginia Union and living in Richmond proved to be a huge culture shock. She often asked herself: "Am I in Hell?" during the ordeal of being arrested and placed in a cell she described as "smelly." She insists that she would do it again, although having the arrest on her record at one time kept her from being hired for a position. Returning to California, she earned a doctorate in psychology from the University of Southern California. Lois White, now Betty White Martin, earned a degree in elementary education at VUU in 1963, went on to earn a master's degree in early childhood education from Virginia Commonwealth University, and embarked on a long teaching career in Boston, Massachusetts. (Both, VUU.)

WOODROW BENJAMIN GRANT JR. AND DONALD VINCENT GOODE. One of the unsung personalities in the Richmond sit-in was Dr. Woodrow Benjamin Grant Jr. (1938–2019). According to his account, he, Sherrod, and Pinkston met on February 6, 1960, to decide on a course of action and called a meeting of students to begin preparations on February 8. Grant's testimony indicates that there was much in the way of meticulous planning for the protest. He continued the struggle for equality as chair of the Maryland State Department of Education Equal Opportunity Office. Donald Vincent Goode (1938–2005) served in the Army until 1964 and moved to Fontana, California, where he worked for many years at Hughes Aircraft Corporation, which later became Raytheon. (Both, VUU.)

RANDOLPH A. TOBIAS AND CAROLYN ANN HORNE BASSETTE. Randolph Allen Tobias earned a doctorate in education and joined the faculty of Queens College at the City University of New York, serving as chair of the Graduate Department of Educational and Community Programs and associate dean for special programs. He is the author of *Ensuring Success in Math and Science: Curriculum and Teaching Strategies for At-Risk Learners*. Carolyn Horne Bassette graduated from Virginia Union with a degree in English education and became a teacher. She first taught at Peabody High School in Petersburg, Virginia; then in Richmond; and ultimately in East Orange, New Jersey, before retiring after nearly 30 years in education. (Both, VUU.)

ROBERT B. DALTON AND FRANCES BARCROFT DALTON. Robert B. Dalton entered the military and rose to the rank of lieutenant colonel in the US Army; he was a bronze star and purple heart recipient. He married a classmate, Frances Jeanette Barcroft, who also happened to be participating in a sit-in, at the Woolworth's lunch counter one block away. Frances Barcroft was one of the leaders of the steering committee that coordinated the continuing student Campaign for Human Dignity protests. They lived in Pine Bluff, Arkansas, where Frances became the owner of Abalone Enterprises, a real estate agency. (Both, VUU.)

LAURA GREENE. Ella Josephine Baker (1903–1986) was one of the true pioneers of the civil rights movement. She began her work with the NAACP in 1938, and in 1957 joined Dr. Martin Luther King Jr.'s Southern Christian Leadership Conference (SCLC). By 1960, she had become dissatisfied with the SCLC and determined to establish a civil rights group that was more democratic and open to women and young people, particularly recent sit-in student leaders. Accordingly, she called a conference to meet at Shaw University in Raleigh, North Carolina, and the Student Nonviolent Coordination Committee (SNCC) was organized. SNCC would become the initiating organization for many of the ensuing civil rights campaigns in the South. Laura Greene, one of the five VUU students/alumni to attend, also served as a leader on the student steering committee of the Campaign for Human Dignity. (VUU.)

Five

THE FORGETTING AND THE REDISCOVERY, TO 2010

The Richmond 34, though long unappreciated, were the catalyst for much of the civil rights advances that followed. Why then, were they forgotten? Perhaps because it was so extraordinarily peaceful? The Richmond sit-in was overshadowed by the violent Nashville incident known as Big Saturday. On February 27, 1960, a total of 81 demonstrators were violently mobbed, then arrested. Larger confrontations loomed that would also capture media attention.

On campus, too, memory faded. The Virginia Union students graduated and moved on to careers, graduate studies, and families. The university administration became wary of the increasingly radicalized political climate during the following years. Militant student groups excoriated the administration for being too moderate and occupied the campus in 1968. With the 1970s shift to a less activist atmosphere and progress on the political front, there was less incentive to invoke a more radical past.

In Richmond, the struggle of the African American community to gain a political voice and controversies involving busing, annexation, and electoral redistricting pushed historical memory of 1960 back even further.

From 2003 to 2004, three threads converged to rekindle awareness of the Richmond sit-in. One was the publication of the first scholarly studies of the event: Dr. Peter Wallenstein's *Blue Laws and Black Codes*, which included an essay "To Sit or Not to Sit," and *Rights for a Season* by Dr. Lewis A. Randolph and Dr. Gayle T. Tate. At Virginia Union, Dr. Raymond Pierre Hylton was researching the 1960 sit-in as part of a project for an institutional history and commemorative events for the 50th anniversary of the *Brown v. the Board of Education* decision. One of the Richmond 34, Elizabeth Patricia Johnson, now Elizabeth Johnson Rice, obtained a permit for a commemorative march down Broad Street to the Thalhimers building. She contacted Dr. Hylton, and the two collaborated on annual commemorative events though 2019.

COBURN HALL RAVAGED BY FIRE. On May 16, 1970, in the early hours of the morning, Coburn Chapel, one of Virginia Union University's original and most revered structures, suddenly ignited and was rapidly engulfed in flames. Though the Virginia granite wall held fast, the interior was destroyed, and it was not restored until 1991. The origin of the blaze is still a controversial topic. The official cause was stated as being electrical in nature, but some, then and now, are of the opinion that it was set by radical elements. This had the effect of further distancing the university administration from the activist occurrences of the 1960s. Coburn Hall, named in 1899 after abolitionist Maine governor Abner Coburn, contains the university chapel and once housed the library collection. (VUU.)

BUSING CONTROVERSY AND DR. MILES J. JONES. The 1971 case of *Bradley v. the Richmond School Board*, in which Judge Robert Merhige mandated school busing to achieve integration, sparked a political firestorm. In the final analysis, the intent was thwarted by "white flight" to suburban jurisdictions and adverse Supreme Court rulings. In 1970, Dr. Miles Jerome Jones, homiletics professor at the Virginia Union School of Theology, was elected to the Richmond City School Board and in 1972 became the board's first African American chair. He served until 1980, and it was said of him: "His quiet and resolute confidence was a unifying force which reassured the city and country that a desegregated school system could work." (Above, RTD; right, VUU.)

FIRST BLACK MAJORITY CITY COUNCIL, 1977. After a long, uphill struggle, the majority of the African American population at last secured proportionate representation. During the 1950s through the 1960s, the white minority, conscious that they were losing ground demographically, clung to an at-large election system for council members to offset the black vote and periodically sought to annex predominately white areas of adjoining counties. From 1972 to 1976, council elections and annexations were suspended by court order and a ward system was mandated for the city. The following year, the voters elected a 5-4 African American majority. The black council members are pictured here: Walter T. Kenney (second from left), Willie J. Dell (third from left), Claudette Black McDaniel (fifth from left), H.W. "Chuck" Richardson (sixth from left), and Henry L. Marsh III (seventh from left). (Richmond City Clerk's Office.)

HENRY L. MARSH III. Graduating from Virginia Union University in 1956 with a bachelor's degree in sociology and a juris doctorate from Howard University Law School in 1959, Henry L. Marsh III began practicing civil rights law as a partner at the firm of Hill, Tucker & Marsh and by 1966 was elected to Richmond City Council. He rose to vice mayor in 1970, and with the election of the first majority African American city council in 1977, he became Richmond's first black mayor, serving in that capacity until 1982. In 1991, he was elected to the Virginia state senate and retired after 23 years in 2014. In 2015, the Manchester District Courthouse in Richmond was named for Marsh and his brother Harold M. Marsh Sr. He published *The Memoirs of Hon. Henry L. Marsh III: Civil Rights Champion, Public Servant, Lawyer* in 2018. (VUU.)

L. Douglas Wilder. The Richmond sit-in began the decade of the 1960s and accelerated the push for civil rights in the entire state of Virginia. One of the most significant spin-offs happened on December 2, 1969, when attorney Lawrence Douglas Wilder won a special election and became the first black state senator in Virginia since Reconstruction. Wilder had graduated from Virginia Union in 1951, served in Korea where he was awarded the Bronze Star for bravery, and attended Howard University Law School. After 16 years as state senator, Wilder was elected Virginia's first black lieutenant governor, serving in that capacity from 1986 to 1990. He was then elected the first black governor of any state, serving from 1990 to 1994. He returned to politics in 2004, becoming Richmond's first black popularly elected mayor, holding office from 2005 to 2009. (VUU.)

Dr. Peter Wallenstein and Blue Laws. From 2003 to 2004, Virginia Tech history professor Peter Wallenstein conducted research with assistance from his former graduate student James R. Clyburn on legal and social changes in Virginia during the 20th century. The results were published in the book *Blue Laws and Black Codes*. One chapter, "To Sit or Not to Sit," dealt with the cases involving the Richmond 34 and with Ford Tucker Johnson Jr.'s contempt of court charges. Dr. Wallenstein earned his doctorate in history at Johns Hopkins University and is also the author of *Tell the Court I Love My Wife* (2002) and *Cradle of America: A History of Virginia* (2007). Dr. Wallenstein has been supportive of initiatives to tell the Richmond 34 story and gave the keynote lecture at the January 22, 2019, MLK Community Week. (Right, Dr. Peter Wallenstein; below, Dr. Kimberly A. Matthews.)

ELIZABETH JOHNSON RICE AND DR. RAYMOND PIERRE HYLTON. In 2000, Elizabeth Johnson Rice narrowly avoided death from an aortic aneurism and reflected on the 1960 events in which she played a crucial role. In 2004, she heard that the Thalhimer Building on Broad Street would be demolished and conceived the idea of holding a commemorative march/rally. Receiving a police permit, she requested support from Virginia Union. At the same time, Dr. Raymond Pierre Hylton, at VUU, was examining the Richmond sit-in as part of a university history project. Directed to Dr. Hylton, Elizabeth Rice phoned him, and the two worked together to rekindle the Richmond 34 story. Pictured above in 2004 are, from left to right, Rice's father, Ford T. Johnson Sr.; her husband, Dr. Richard Rice; Rice; and her sister Phyllis Johnson Richardson. (Both, Dr. Raymond Pierre Hylton.)

THE 2004 COMMEMORATION. In honor of the 50th anniversary of the *Brown v. the Board of Education* decision, programs were held at Virginia Union. The special guest lecturer was Charles Melvin Sherrod (seated at right above). Since his graduation from Virginia Union University, Sherrod had accomplished much of note. He participated in the 1961 freedom rides with fellow VUU graduates Obadiah Simms, Raymond B. Randolph Jr., and Reginald M. Green. In October 1961, he initiated and directed the Albany (Georgia) civil rights movement, which raged on through August 1962. He returned to Albany and served on its city council from 1976 to 1990. Dr. Laverne Byrd Smith (at left below with Dr. Delores Greene, second from left), who had been instrumental in raising the bail money for the 34, was a welcome guest. (Both, VUU.)

THE TWO ELIZABETHS AND FINDING THALHIMERS. During the 2004 march to the old Thalhimers building, Elizabeth Rice made the acquaintance of Elizabeth Thalhimer Smartt, the granddaughter of William Blum Thalhimer Jr. The two became friends, and since they were both Elizabeths, they referred to each other as "Little E" (Smartt, above left) and "Big E" (Rice, above right). Elizabeth Thalhimer Smartt earned a master's degree in English from Virginia Commonwealth University and in 2010 published *Finding Thalhimers*, which related the history of her family's famous department store and includes accounts of the 1960 sit-in and her meeting with Elizabeth Johnson Rice. (Above, Elizabeth Johnson Rice; left, Dr. Kimberly A. Matthews.)

Six

THE 34/50 COMMEMORATION AND BEYOND, 2010–2019

In 2010, CenterStage in Richmond joined Virginia Union in staging a weeklong program celebrating the 50th anniversary of the arrest of the 34. The organizing committee located and brought to campus either the actual individuals or relatives of 27 out of the 34. Two stone monuments were erected: one on the VUU campus at Martin E. Gray Hall and the other at the site of the former Thalhimers. John Legend was brought in to perform in honor of the occasion.

On March 4, 2016, at the Virginia Forum held in Williamsburg, Virginia, Dr. Raymond Hylton delivered a paper in which he urged that action be taken on the erection of a state historical marker at the former Thalhimers site, which had been in the works since 2009. The response was supportive, and on June 28, 2016, the marker was placed in the middle of the block of Broad Street between Sixth and Seventh Streets, with four of the 34 members in attendance.

In 2018, when Dr. Anderson J. Franklin applied for a passport, the Department of Homeland Security informed him that the criminal arrest against him and his fellow Richmond 34 members was still on their record. Judge Birdie Hairston Jamison set out to rectify this long-standing injustice. Virginia Union University president Dr. Hakim J. Lucas organized a special committee to hold events on January 22 and February 21–22, 2019, celebrating the 59th anniversary of the sit-in and the expungement of the arrest records. On February 21, 2019, Virginia governor Ralph Northam and First Lady Pamela Northam invited the Richmond 34 and planning committee members to breakfast at the Governor's Mansion to mark the anniversary. This was followed by a resolution introduced in the Virginia General Assembly by delegate Delores McQuinn honoring the 34, then a panel discussion at the Virginia Union campus, and finally a journey to the district court, where those of the 34 members in attendance had their arrest records expunged.

Plans are under way to celebrate the 60th anniversary in 2020.

RICHMOND CENTERSTAGE/DOMINION ENERGY CENTER AND 34 VIDEO. In 2004, the Thalhimers building was demolished, and the site was merged with that of the Carpenter Center Theater on Grace Street to create the Richmond CenterStage complex (most of the site occupied by the former department store was converted into the theater parking lot). The complex was organized to foster the performing arts. In 2010, the Richmond CenterStage Foundation collaborated with Virginia Union University to hold events commemorating the 50th anniversary of the Richmond sit-in. In 2015, the complex was renamed the Dominion Energy Center. As part of the commemorative activities, CenterStage interviewed some of the 34 to produce the first video documentary of the event: *Sit-In Stand Out*. (Above, Dr. Kimberly A. Matthews; left, Richmond Performing Arts Alliance.)

34/50 COMMEMORATION POSTER AND KEY RING. The 50th anniversary events were coordinated at the Virginia Union campus and CenterStage sites by a special program committee chaired by Dr. Raymond Pierre Hylton. The blanket term under which the celebratory programs, which were held from February 22 to 26, 2010, was "34/50." Among the pamphlets, brochures, and posters designed and produced for the events was this one, which listed all the names of the 34 students arrested, encircled by photographs of 24 of them, surmounted by the motto: "Dauntless and uncompromising in their quest for freedom." Even key rings were custom-made for the occasion. (Right, VUU; below, Dr. Kimberly A. Matthews.)

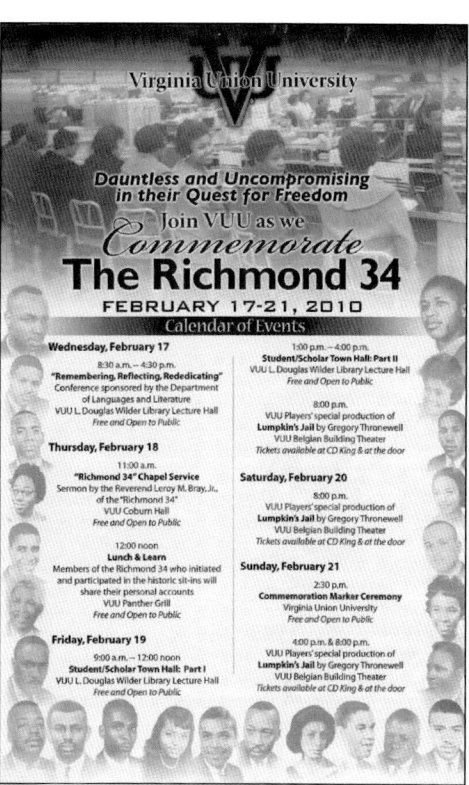

MORE FROM 34/50 ACTIVITIES. Easily the oldest individual at the commemoration was Wesley Carter Sr. (1907–2012, above center), a Virginia Union graduate from the class of 1929, who was 102 years old at the time. Here he stands with, from left to right, Monique Nero, VUU president Claude G. Perkins, Barbara Thornton Nero, Frances Barcroft Dalton, Robin Nero Pearson, and Robert V. Nero. Carter was instrumental in helping to erect a statue to the Richmond-born entertainer Bill "Bojangles" Robinson in 1973 at Adams and Leigh Streets. Below is a photograph of 34/50 attendees with VUU president Claude G. Perkins (seventh from right). (Both, VUU.)

JOHN LEGEND CONCERT AND *UNIONITE* ISSUE. The John Legend concert on the evening of February 22, 2010, capped the Richmond 34 celebration activities. Legend, whose name is John Roger Stephens, was born on December 28, 1978, long after the Richmond sit-in, but he derived inspiration from their courage and initiative. His program, "An Evening of Reflection," was performed at CenterStage. On the same evening, Richmond City Council passed a resolution honoring the 34. The Virginia Union University magazine *Unionite* printed a special issue with photographs of 34 members on the cover. (Both, VUU.)

PRODUCTION OF LUMPKIN'S JAIL. Among the events of the 34/50 week was the production of the play *Lumpkin's Jail*, which was directed by VUU drama instructor L. Roi Boyd. The play, written by Virginia Union graduate Gregory Thornewell, depicts the events surrounding the university's founding. Among the historical figures portrayed were Mary F. Lumpkin, Dr. Nathaniel and Gloria Colver, and Dr. Charles Henry Corey. There was added interest to the story because of the well-publicized archeological excavation of the Lumpkin's Jail site in 2006 by the James River Institute for Archaeology, which uncovered the foundations of the old jail. (Above, VUU; below, Monique Nero.)

LARRY WOODSON AND THE SIXTH STREET MONUMENT STONE. Larry Woodson, a 1974 graduate of Virginia Union University who was very active in alumni affairs and fundraising and served as president of the Coach Thomas Harris Alumni Chapter, spoke to Tony Grappone, the proprietor of A.P. Grappone & Sons stone carvers, and Grappone agreed to carve and donate two stone monuments to honor the Richmond 34. One of these was placed on Sixth Street between Broad and Grace Streets at the site of the old Thalhimers building. Above, Woodson is seen with Barbara Thornton Nero. (Above, Monique Nero; below, Dr. Kimberly A. Matthews.)

CAMPUS MONUMENT STONE. A.P. Grappone & Sons was founded in 1910 by Alfonso Grappone, from Paternopoli, Italy, and has been handed down for four generations, from Alfonso to his great-grandson Tony, and has operated out of the same building on Randolph Street near Hollywood Cemetery all those years. The inscription on the stone was written by Dr. Raymond Pierre Hylton and contains the names of the 34 with a verse from Matthew 5:6, "Blessed are they who hunger and thirst for justice, for they shall be satisfied." (Both, Dr. Kimberly A. Matthews.)

DEDICATION OF CAMPUS MONUMENT STONE. On Sunday, February 21, 2010, the campus stone honoring the Richmond 34 was unveiled and dedicated in front of the Martin E. Gray Hall and behind the restored Coburn Chapel (below). This venue was chosen because it was the site of the assemblage of students prior to their march to the downtown shopping district in 1960. As several Richmond 34 members and their families clustered around, dedicatory speeches were delivered by university president Dr. Claude Grandford Perkins and Dr. Raymond Pierre Hylton. (Above, VUU; below, Dr. Kimberly A. Matthews.)

THE 150TH ANNIVERSARY MONUMENT. In 2015, Virginia Union University celebrated the 150th anniversary of its founding, which effectively occurred on April 3, 1865, with the Union army's liberation of Richmond. One of the highlights of the commemoration activities was the dedication of the 150th anniversary monument on campus. Designed by sculptor Ed Dwight of Denver, the monument includes six panels illustrating salient events in the university's history. In the fifth panel, the Richmond 34 was acknowledged with the inclusion of the photograph of Frank George Pinkston's arrest. (Both, Dr. Kimberly A. Matthews.)

THE BROAD STREET HISTORICAL MARKER. Virginia State Historical markers were proposed in 2009–2010 to highlight events pertinent to African American, Native American, and women's history themes, which would include one for the Richmond 34. In 2016, all was ready, and June 28, 2016, was scheduled as the dedication date. The marker was to be erected mid-block on Broad Street between Sixth and Seventh Streets. CenterStage/Dominion Energy agreed to facilitate the ceremony and provided room space for the organizers and guests prior to the event, which was coordinated by Elizabeth Rice and Dr. Raymond Pierre Hylton. (Dr. Kimberly A. Matthews.)

DEDICATION OF THE BROAD STREET MARKER. At the appointed time of 12:00 noon, the Richmond 34 members present, accompanied by family members, were led to the Dominion Energy center parking lot by Scottish pipe master Fay Hylton King, who played "Highland Cathedral" in their honor. There were short speeches by Elizabeth Johnson Rice, Dr. Raymond Pierre Hylton, and Dr. Stephanie Latrice Hooks (a Virginia Union alumna and public schoolteacher who had assisted at the 2004 march to the Thalhimers building). The above photograph shows the moment that Ford Tucker Johnson Jr. unveiled the marker; at left are Dr. Hylton and his cousin Fay Hylton King. (Above, RTD; left, the Hylton family.)

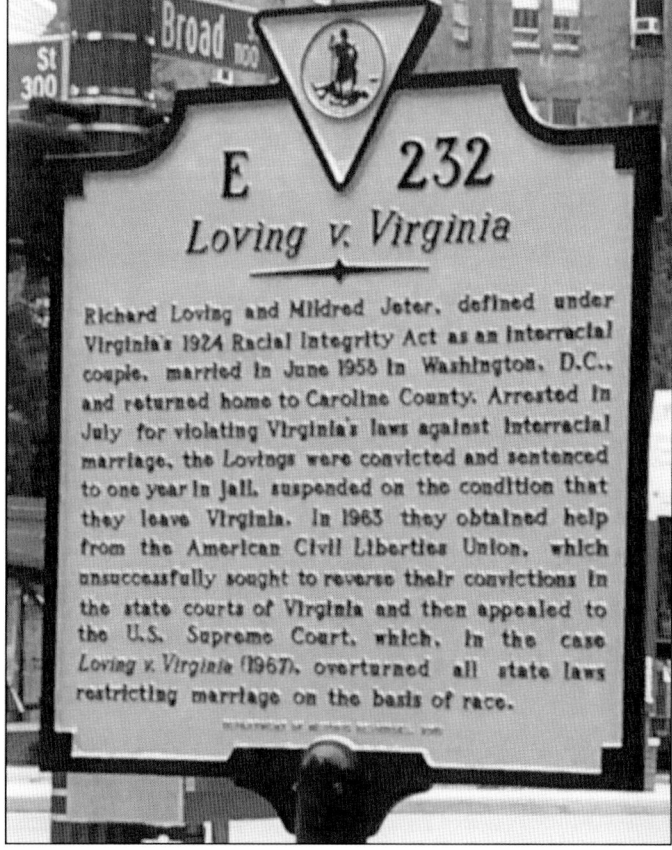

MONUMENTS NEAR THE BROAD STREET MARKER. The marker on Broad Street was a welcome addition to historical monuments and markers that have been erected over the years to offer to both visitors and Richmonders a more well-rounded view of the city's history, culture, and traditions. A few blocks to the west on Adams and Broad Streets is a statue and monument stones erected in honor of the African American banker Maggie Lena Walker. To the east, on Broad and Eleventh Streets, is a marker memorializing the case of *Loving v. Virginia*, in which the Supreme Court ruled laws prohibiting interracial marriages to be unconstitutional. (Above, Brianna Scott; right, Dr. Kimberly A. Matthews.)

DR. A.J. FRANKLIN AND SIT-IN CHILDREN'S BOOK. In 2018, Dr. Anderson J. Franklin (above at center with Elizabeth Johnson Rice) prepared to leave the country for a trip abroad when, amazingly, his passport application was denied because of his criminal record. Although the Supreme Court had reversed the conviction, his arrest record had not been expunged. Franklin contacted Elizabeth Rice, who discovered that this was indeed the case for all 34. Rice contacted the NAACP, which asked Judge Birdie Hairston Jamison to resolve the matter. At the same time, a children's book was released, written by Habibah Quddus (with Elizabeth Johnson Rice) about the Richmond 34 and was entitled *Sit-In and Stand Out*. It related the Richmond 34 events from Rice's perspective. (Above, Clyde Bradly; below, Dr. Kimberly A. Matthews.)

JUDGE BIRDIE HAIRSTON JAMISON. Judge Jamison attended the College of William and Mary, graduating with a bachelor's degree in business administration in 1979 and with a juris doctor degree in 1982. In 1991, she was appointed the judge presiding over the 13th Judicial District (Traffic) Court of Virginia, serving until her retirement in 2015. With 24 years on the bench, she held the longest tenure of office of any traffic court judge. She served on the National Advisory Board of the Hardcore Drunk Driving Judicial Education Project. When it came to the attention of the NAACP that the arrest convictions of members of the Richmond 34 were still on their records, Judge Jamison was called upon to remedy this injustice and navigate through the legal process to accomplish this in time for the 59th anniversary of the Richmond sit-in. (VUU.)

JANUARY–FEBRUARY 2019 EVENTS. The 59th anniversary commemoration began with the formation of a committee by Virginia Union president Dr. Hakim J. Lucas, who first organized a special program on campus on January 22, 2019, which featured Dr. Peter Wallenstein speaking on "the continuing impact of *Raymond B. Randolph, Jr,* and *Johnson vs. Virginia*" and Judge Birdie Hairston Jamison on "implications of racial discrimination in the Richmond courts." Shown above are, from left to right, Janith Libron, Dr. Hylton, Elizabeth Rice, Judge Jamison, and Dr. Wallenstein. A university-sponsored "Faith, Identity, and Social Justice" program took place on February 21, 2019, at Coburn Chapel and the following day at the Claude G. Perkins Living & Learning Center. Below, Dr. A.J. Franklin (left) and Wendell T. Foster Jr. are pictured with the Virginia Union band playing in the background. (Both, VUU.)

"Faith, Identity, and Social Justice" Panel. The February 22, 2019, "Faith, Identity, and Social Justice" event at the Claude G. Perkins Living & Learning Center included a panel discussion with six panelists. They are, from left to right, Judge Birdie Hairston Jamison, Dr. Raymond Pierre Hylton, Dr. Anderson J. Franklin, Dr. Leroy M. Bray Jr., Ford Tucker Johnson Jr., and Elizabeth Johnson Rice. The photograph below provides a view of the audience in attendance. What became obvious as the recollections and discussions unfolded was how far certain human rights had progressed but also how far people are from realizing Dr. King's community in other respects. (Both, VUU.)

EXIT PROCESSION. Out of the original Richmond 34, twelve are known to have passed away, and five more have, to date, not been located. Like the earlier World War II generation, those who were involved in the civil rights struggle are also being whittled away through the passage of time. There is, then, an even greater sense of urgency to preserve historical memory by recognizing and relating their stories and those of others whose contributions have yet to be told. At left, following the event at the Claude G. Perkins Living & Learning Center, Fred Pinkston, representing his late brother Frank, proudly holds a copy of the General Assembly resolution. Below are Ford Tucker Johnson Jr. and his sister Elizabeth Johnson Rice. (Both, VUU.)

GOVERNOR'S INVITATION. Gov. Ralph Northam of Virginia became enmeshed in controversy when it was revealed that his page in the 1984 Eastern Virginia Medical School yearbook contained a photograph showing one man wearing blackface and another in Ku Klux Klan robes. The governor attested that neither of the men was him. As part of initiating reconciliation efforts, the governor was scheduled to appear at the Richmond 34 chapel services on February 21. When the president of the Student Government Association protested and the appearance was cancelled, Elizabeth Rice objected that the governor should be involved, and the 34 members and those on the Commemoration Committee were invited for breakfast at the Governor's Mansion on the morning of February 22. Pictured above are, from left to right, Governor Northam, Judge Jamison, Dr. A.J. Franklin, and Elizabeth Rice. Below, First Lady Pamela Northam and the governor greet those assembled. (Both, GOV.)

GOVERNOR'S BREAKFAST. Four members of the Richmond 34 were able to attend, plus a veteran of the sit-in who was not among those arrested, Janith Libron. The governor, standing at left above, addressed those attending the breakfast. Below, standing with Governor Northam and holding copies of the impending General Assembly resolution, are, from left to right, Amirah Salaam; Dr. Leroy M. Bray Jr.; Dr. Anderson J. Franklin; Elizabeth Johnson Rice; Wendall T. Foster Jr., and Janith Libron. Someone present was heard to remark: "Harry F. Byrd Sr. must be turning in his grave." (Both, GOV.)

DELEGATE DELORES MCQUINN AND ASSEMBLY RESOLUTION. Delegate Delores L. McQuinn (at microphone) attended both Virginia Union University and Virginia Commonwealth University. She first entered the political stage in 1992, when she was elected to the Richmond City School Board and served until 1996. Three years later, she won election to the Richmond City Council. On January 6, 2009, running on the Democratic ticket, she won a special election for the 70th District House of Delegates seat. On February 22, 2019, McQuinn introduced a resolution recognizing the 59th anniversary of the Richmond 34. She is seen above with Dr. A.J. Franklin, Elizabeth Johnson Rice, Dr. Leroy M. Bray Jr., and Wendell T. Foster Jr., among others. (Above, VUU; right, Dr. Kimberly A. Matthews.)

AT THE GENERAL ASSEMBLY. Immediately following the governor's breakfast, delegate Delores McQuinn introduced the Richmond 34 recognition resolution, which passed the General Assembly. The irony of the occasion was not lost: The 1960 General Assembly, after the arrest of the 34, toughened the anti-trespassing law penalty, mandating a minimum $1,000 fine and/or 12 months' imprisonment. The above photograph shows delegate Delores McQuinn holding the resolution. From left to right behind here are Elizabeth Johnson Rice, Dr. Anderson J. Franklin, Dr. Leroy M. Bray Jr., and Wendell T. Foster Jr.. Below, under the gaze of Jean-Antoine Houdon's statue of George Washington, those assembled beam in triumph. (Both, VUU.)

EXPUNGING THE CRIMINAL ARREST RECORDS. On February 22, 2019, after the "Faith, Identity, and Social Justice" event at Virginia Union, the official expungement process occurred at the Richmond Courthouse. There, with Judge Birdie Hairston Jamison (above, first row, seated at right) advocating their case, five members of the Richmond 34 were fingerprinted and had their trespassing arrest records expunged. They are pictured below, from left to right (beginning third from left), Ford Tucker Johnson Jr., Dr. Leroy M. Bray Jr., Dr. Anderson J. Franklin, Elizabeth Johnson Rice, and Wendall T. Foster Jr. (Both, VUU.)

Dr. King at VUU and Dr. Leroy M. Bray Jr. in 2019. The continuing saga of the 1960 sit-ins, with the arrest of the Richmond 34 in the former capital of the Confederacy and the bastion of the Byrd Machine playing a significant historical role, offers a sobering lesson. That is, within living memory, rights that are currently taken as a matter of course were often blatantly denied and could be again, and that freedom involves constant struggle. It is appropriate that the story pauses with the words of two individuals: one who was the greatest source of inspiration for those 34 students nearly six decades back, and the other who was the first of those called to act upon that inspiration. Dr. Martin Luther King Jr. stated, "Injustice anywhere is a threat to justice everywhere." And Dr. Leroy M. Bray Jr. said, "Forget the hatred, but remember the history." (Both, VUU.)

Bibliography

Belsches, Elvatrice Parker. *Richmond, Virginia*. Charleston, SC: Arcadia Publishing, 2002.
Daugherity, Brian J. *Keep on Keeping On: The NAACP and the Implementation of Brown v. Board of Education in Virginia*. Charlottesville, VA: University of Virginia Press, 2016.
Edds, Margaret. *We Face the Dawn: Oliver Hill, Spottswood Robinson and the Legal Team that Dismantled Jim Crow*. Charlottesville, VA: University of Virginia Press, 2018.
Hylton, Raymond Pierre. *Virginia Union University*. Charleston, SC: Arcadia Publishing, 2014.
McAdam, Doug. *Political Process and the Development of Black Insurgency, 1930–1970*. Chicago, IL: The University of Chicago Press, 1982.
Matthews, Kimberly A. *The Richmond Crusade for Voters*. Charleston, SC: Arcadia Publishing, 2017.
Oppenheimer, Martin. *The Sit-In Movement of 1960*. Brooklyn, NY: Carlson Publishing, 1989.
Peeples, Edward H. *Scalawag: A White Southerner's Journey through Segregation to Human Rights Activism*. Charlottesville, VA: University of Virginia Press, 2017.
Randolph, Lewis A., and Gayle T. Tate. *Rights for a Season: The Politics of Race, Class, and Gender in Richmond, Virginia*. Knoxville, TN: University of Tennessee Press, 2003.
Schmidt, Christopher W. *The Sit-Ins: Protest & Legal Change in the Civil Right Era*. Chicago, IL: The University of Chicago Press, 2018.
Silver, Christopher, and John V. Moeser. *The Separate City: Black Communities in the Urban South 1940–1968*. Lexington, KY: The University Press of Kentucky, 1995.
Smartt, Elizabeth Thalhimer. *Finding Thalhimers*. Manakin-Sabot, VA: Dementi Milestone Publishing, 2010.
Wallenstein, Peter. *Blue Laws and Black Codes: Conflict, Courts, and Change in Twentieth-Century Virginia*. Charlottesville, VA: University of Virginia Press, 2004.
Wilson, Jamie J. *Civil Rights Movement*. Santa Barbara, CA: Greenwood ABC-CLIO, 2013.

Discover Thousands of Local History Books
Featuring Millions of Vintage Images

Arcadia Publishing, the leading local history publisher in the United States, is committed to making history accessible and meaningful through publishing books that celebrate and preserve the heritage of America's people and places.

Find more books like this at
www.arcadiapublishing.com

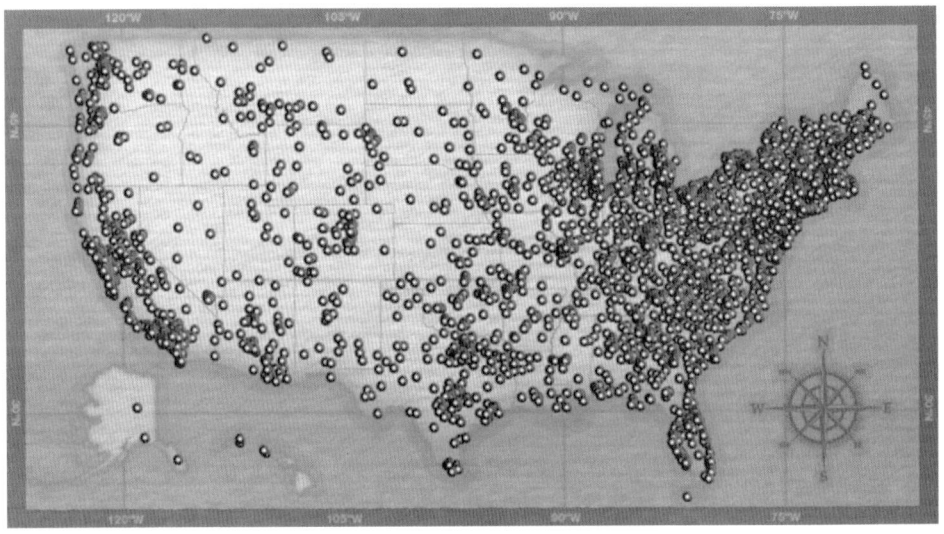

Search for your hometown history, your old stomping grounds, and even your favorite sports team.

Consistent with our mission to preserve history on a local level, this book was printed in South Carolina on American-made paper and manufactured entirely in the United States. Products carrying the accredited Forest Stewardship Council (FSC) label are printed on 100 percent FSC-certified paper.